Christians and Muslims Together

Christians and Muslims Together

An Exploration by Presbyterians

Edited by
Byron L. Haines and Frank L. Cooley

The Geneva Press
Philadelphia

Book design by Gene Harris

First edition

Published by The Geneva Press®
Philadelphia, Pennsylvania

PRINTED IN THE UNITED STATES OF AMERICA

9 8 7 6 5 4 3 2 1

Library of Congress Cataloging-in-Publication Data

Christians and Muslims together.

   Bibliography: p.
   1. Islam—Relations—Christianity.   2. Christianity and other religions—Islam.   I. Haines, Byron.
II. Cooley, Frank L. (Frank Leonard), 1920–
BP172.C42 1987   261.2'7   87-218
ISBN 0-664-24061-5 (pbk.)

Contents

Preface

At dawn each morning across the world over nine hundred million people are awakened by a call to prayer. "Come to prayer. Come to prayer. Prayer is better than sleep. God is great!" The faithful respond, for they know that the obedient life is one that prayer nourishes and God rewards. In the daily ritual of prayer they demonstrate to the world that they are Muslims, those who worship God in the religion of Islam.

There are many reasons why Christians in the West need to take seriously not only this religion but also the peoples who find in it that which makes life possible, and the civilization it has produced. Current events have moved the concerns of Muslim peoples to the center of the stage. The Islamic revolution in Iran, the Palestinian–Israeli conflict and its effects in the Middle East, and references made by the media to an Islamic resurgence in the world are but a few such examples.

The impact of the Muslim world on the West is more than political events in the Middle East. There is a growing economic interdependence between Muslim nations and the United States. In 1973 Americans became aware of how much they were dependent upon oil from Saudi Arabia. Trade and industrial ties with Muslim nations are a major source of income for many U.S. companies. The Christian church in the United States has through its mission programs been involved with Muslim peoples for over 150 years. This Christian presence has not been well received by Muslims for reasons that Christians need to ponder.

Finally, Christians in the United States are gradually becoming aware of the presence of a substantial Muslim community in the United States as Islamic centers and mosques are found all over the country, not only in the larger cities but in such locations as Abiquiu, New Mexico; Cedar Rapids, Iowa; and Christiansburg, Virginia. These reflect the growing size and vitality of the Islamic presence in America. In addition to the Muslim citizens who support these centers, tens of thousands of Muslim students from overseas are enrolled in universities and colleges in the United States.

What have been the responses to all these circumstances? In many cases the responses have been negative. There is a growing prejudice in the United States against Islam and Muslims. This prejudice has been nourished by a variety of causes, but the major ones are ignorance and fear. Instead of giving in to prejudice, which inevitably corrupts all human relationships, the time has come for Christians to respond to the presence of their Muslim neighbors in new ways and with new attitudes. This book is an attempt to suggest what those new ways and attitudes might be and how they might come about.

Our aim is to provide reliable information about Islam and the Muslim world, to examine the relationships between Muslims and Christians in several countries, and to explore together the nature and direction of future associations in the pluralistic world of today. The specific objectives of the study invite Christians:

• To review and rethink their approach to Islam and their relation to Muslims
• To overcome their prejudices toward and stereotypes about Islam, Muslims, and Arabs
• To reexamine and clarify their attitudes, motivations, and intentions in regard to interfaith relations in general and relations with Muslims in particular
• To engage in more creative and fresh theological and missiological thinking concerning the mission of the church in today's pluralistic world

In 1983 the General Assembly Mission Board (GAMB) of the Presbyterian Church (U.S.A.) approved undertaking a study of the Islamic world and Christian–Muslim relations, an action in which the Program Agency later concurred. The study was designed and implemented by Frank L. Cooley, staff person appointed by the Division of International Mission of the GAMB, with the assistance of Edward M. Huenemann of the Program Agency. The work was monitored and assisted by an Islamic Study Advisory Committee (ISAC) appointed in early 1984, with Joyce C. Stark as chair. As the study progressed, ISAC became a working committee, with every member undertaking parts of the study and evaluating the results. The twelve members were David H. Bowman, Donald G. Dawe, William G. Gepford, Yvonne Y. Haddad, Bing Kong Han, C. Eric Lincoln, Victor E. Makari, Joyce C. Stark, Morton S. Taylor, Otis Turner, Margaret O. Thomas, and J. Dudley Woodberry. They were joined in 1986 by Thomas M. Norwood and J. Paul Frelick. Byron L. Haines, Co-Director of the Office on Christian-Muslim Relations of the National Council of the Churches of Christ in the U.S.A., served the committee as consultant and Lawrence R. Richards served as missionary-in-residence staff. The committee members are ruling elders, pastors, and missionaries who have served in Muslim lands, along with specialists in Islamic studies, evangelism, theology, and the sociology of religion.

In 1986 the General Assembly of the Presbyterian Church (U.S.A.) took action to receive in 1987 a report with recommendations concerning Christian–Muslim relations. With that immediate obligation in mind, the advisory committee decided that a book such as this would be a helpful guide for the commissioners to the 1987 General Assembly as they deliberate on the report, as well as for all Christians. The outline and content of this book and the processes leading to its publishing were determined by ISAC. Dr. Byron Haines and Dr. Frank Cooley were asked to serve as its editors.

At the beginning of each chapter, a footnote lists the name of the contributor. Chapters 2, 3, and 4 are condensations of full reports on the major topics of those chapters. Muslim sources were used as much as possible. A Lebanon case study was planned, but circumstances have ruled out its completion and inclusion here. The case studies in chapter 4 are based on data collected mainly by field research, though written sources were also used. Chapters 5 and 6 represent analyses of the materials found in preceding sections.

The editors wish to thank the members of the committee and R. Marston Speight, Sara Burress, and Barbara H. Haines for their help with the editing process.

A brief study guide has been prepared by Margaret O. Thomas, for those who wish to use this book in group study. It can be ordered from the Office of Education for Ecumenism, 1144 Interchurch Center, 475 Riverside Drive, New York, NY 10115-0050; (212) 870-2581.

1

A Summary of the Faith
and Practice of Islam

In spite of a long history of association, the Christian church and most of its members have very little understanding of Islam and the Muslim world. Today this situation is not helped by the prejudice against and stereotypes of Islam and Muslims that appear regularly in media reports of events in the Middle East. If Christians wish to be true to their own religious principles, they must seek to understand as fully as possible the religion of Islam and the people who live by its tenets. What follows here is a concise overview of the faith and practices of Islam, intended to help overcome some of this misunderstanding. It is inadequate not only because of its conciseness but also because it is a Christian's summary of another religious tradition. Some of the terminology used to describe Islamic beliefs is not Islamic, but it is used because it will convey more clearly to Christian readers that which traditional Islam intends. It is hoped that this brief introduction will encourage readers to pursue additional studies in cooperation with Muslim friends and neighbors.

The Worship of God

At the heart of Islam is the worship of God. No other world religion is more concerned than Islam to give God due regard in every aspect of human life. The Arabic word *islam* means

---

This chapter was written by Byron L. Haines.

"submission." It is submission to the will of God, not because of obligations due God, or because of a fear of God, but because the believer is thankful to God for the divine grace and mercy that has made life possible. The word *Muslim* designates the one who practices or is the doer of Islam. Muslims believe that the God whom they worship (the Arabic word for God is *Allah*) is the same God worshiped by Jews and Christians. This is the God of Abraham, the same God whose self-revelation was given through the prophets beginning with Adam and continuing through Moses, Jesus, and finally Muhammad.

In speaking about God, Muslims use the phrase, "I bear witness that there is no God but God and that Muhammad is his messenger." In this phrase God's unity *(tawhid)* is emphasized. God is one. God is not begotten and does not beget. Given the idolatry of Mecca during the time of the Prophet Muhammad, this was a revolutionary affirmation. The unity of God asserts the transcendence of God as the creator of the world. God's unity encompasses all that has happened in the past, all that is taking place in the present, and all that will take place in the future. Nothing can be compared to God. Nothing is like God. The greatest sin in Islam is therefore *shirk*, or "association"—the act of putting someone or something on a par with or ahead of God. All idolatry is rejected. Muslims reject also any anthropomorphic representation in religious practice and art lest that become a substitute for God. To abrogate the unity of God is to deny that God is the omnipotent, omniscient creator, the lord and sovereign ruler of all worlds.

The transcendent unity of God does not, however, mean that God is remote to the believer. God is always active in the world through acts of mercy and grace. Life therefore always has purpose and meaning because God's compassion and providential care are constantly supporting and guiding it. One phrase that is always in the mind and heart of the believer and that begins every chapter of the Qur'an, the holy book of the Muslims (with one exception), is, "In the name of God, the merciful, the compassionate." A more literal translation would be "God, the compassionate compassionator." The very nature of God is merciful and compassionate. This nature leads God to act always with mercy and compassion toward the creation. By the mercy of God, human beings were created with free will so each person is accountable only for his or her own wrongdoing. On the day of final judgment, when each person is held accountable before God, even there God's mercy will prevail so that salvation cannot be earned by human effort but rather is ultimately dependent upon the mercy of God.

Muslims live with a strong sense of their dependence upon God's compassion, and they try to live their lives as an expression of thanksgiving for God's grace toward them. This thanksgiving is found in the phrase that permeates all Muslim prayer, "God is great," and in the ritual use of the "Ninety-nine Names" of God, words that describe God's nature and the character of God's active will in creation. God is the "forgiver," "lover," "judge," "provider," "sustainer," "doer"— to list a few of these names. Using a string of thirty-three beads in three cycles, Muslims recite these names as an act of devotion to God. In the whole of Muslim tradition, there are over five hundred such names. This is of no particular importance because there is always the additional name which is unknown, reminding the believer that no human terminology can grasp in any way the divine majesty and character of God. People are finite; God is infinite. By using these phrases in their devotional life, Muslims remember that God is near to them in mercy and that all of life is dependent upon God.

Islam is, therefore, the worship of God. All human effort should witness to God and God's sovereignty over life now and life to come. True worship consists in being faithful to what God has willed, lest one should be tempted to place loyalty elsewhere. For this reason, to be faithful one must know what the will of God is. In this search for the will of God, the Muslim turns to the holy book, the Qur'an.

The Qur'an, the Revelation from God

How has the will of this transcendent God been made known by God to the world? The Islamic answer is the Qur'an, which is the Word of God. The word *Qur'an* means "recitation" or "reading." It refers directly to the manner of revelation. God is understood to have "recited," from an eternal, preexistent, heavenly book, that which was appropriate to the occasion. This recitation was taken by the angel Gabriel and placed in the mouth of the Prophet Muhammad, who in turn recited God's words for all to hear. Upon hearing, it was written down and checked for accuracy. These writings were then collected to form the Qur'an. As a result, Muslims believe that the Qur'an contains the exact words, recorded and transmitted without error, that God spoke in heaven. It is in every respect literally the Word and words of God, a divinely revealed scripture, in no way corrupted by human error.

A number of other concepts flow from this understanding of the origin of the Qur'an. Because it is God's Word, the Qur'an is without error. That which disagrees with it is, ipso facto, wrong. Though Muslims believe that God has given revelations to earlier prophets, specifically to Moses in the Law, to David in the Psalms, and to Jesus in the Gospels, nevertheless these earlier writings have been so corrupted by Jews and Christians that they have validity only when they confirm that which the Qur'an maintains. In areas of difference, the inerrancy of the Qur'an prevails. To believe otherwise would be to attribute error to God, which is to dishonor God.

These beliefs concerning the Qur'an underscore the purpose of the Qur'an in the life of the believer. It is God's divine guidance for all of life, given by God for all people for all time, so that people will know how to live faithfully. All the moral and ethical principles people need in order to have a just and equitable world and ensure God's blessing and favor upon human endeavors and associations are found in the Qur'an. The importance of this to Muslims should never be underestimated, because those who follow the divine path given in the Qur'an will surely in God's mercy find salvation now and in the life to come.

Because the Qur'an is the literal word of God, it must be recited and studied in Arabic, the language of revelation. This "Arabicity" of the Qur'an prevents it from being translated, if by translation one implies that the meaning of the original can be presented without error or distortion in another language.

The best that one can hope for are paraphrases, which must always be checked against the Arabic original. For this reason, in the paraphrases of the Qur'an published by Muslims, the original Arabic text is always present and takes priority over the paraphrase. Further, the Arabic of the Qur'an testifies to its miraculous character. There is no other Arabic like it. All this means that any serious study of the Qur'an and Islam must begin with a knowledge of the Arabic language of the Qur'an. In this way one has the best hope of understanding God's will without error.

The Qur'an, as a book, consists of 114 chapters or Surahs, each Surah containing verses called *ayat,* or "signs" of God. The Surahs are not in the order in which the revelation was received. In general, the longer Surahs were revealed in Medina; the shorter, in Mecca. (These two cities will be discussed later.) The Surah used most in prayer is the first, Surah Fatihah. To know and follow these verses is to be a Muslim. Surrounding these Qur'anic particulars is the ultimate value of the Qur'an's message of guidance. It is God's miracle, incapable of being imitated, self-authenticating, sublime in its form and content. For Muslims, it is the words of God, which, when obeyed, bring eternal life.

The Prophethood of Muhammad

Crucial to an adequate understanding of Islam is an appreciation of the role of the Prophet Muhammad. Muslims believe that God's self-revealing will has been given by God to prophets, each people having its own prophet who spoke on God's behalf the revelation appropriate for that people in that time. So while Islam accepts most of the prophets of the Bible as authentic speakers for God, it affirms that Muhammad, the Prophet of God, is above them all. Unlike the earlier prophets (and anyone after him who might claim to be a prophet), he came to *all* peoples and nations. The revelations which God gave to him are of timeless value and importance for life and have been preserved without error. For these reasons no other prophets after Muhammad are needed or recognized by Islam, and earlier prophetic revelations need not be consulted.

Muhammad is the last and the greatest of the prophets, one who has truly spoken on God's behalf and has truly embodied in his own life the full meaning and intent of that revelation. As a result, not only has the Qur'an been preserved but also all records of the Prophet's words and deeds (that is, the Prophet's *sunnah,* or "path") have been collected into a body of literature known as the *hadith,* which is consulted after the Qur'an as a major source for determining God's will.

Muhammad (A.D. 570–632) was born in Mecca, the commercial and cultural center of the Arabian peninsula at that time. At the age of forty he began to receive revelations from God which he recited to the people of Mecca. Many of these early revelations were warnings about God's judgment upon the pagan religious practices and the social injustices that characterized life in Mecca. These revelations called the people to repent of their evil ways and to return to the worship of the one true God. Such announcements earned Muhammad the wrath of those in Mecca who maintained their positions of power and authority by means of these evil conditions. When all appeared to be lost, the Prophet received from the people of Yathrib, a city some two hundred miles to the north of Mecca, an invitation for him and his small group of followers to come and exercise leadership in their city. The invitation was accepted as a vindication from God. Muhammad and his followers emigrated to Yathrib in 622. This emigration is known to Muslims as the Hijrah, an event so important that it marks the first day of the Muslim calendar. In Yathrib, Islam took root and eventually expanded to encompass the city of Mecca and the whole of the Arabian peninsula. Yathrib became known as Medina—that is, "the city" (of Muhammad)— and Mecca became the religious center for Islam, followed closely in importance by Medina, the administrative center, and Jerusalem, the city from which the Prophet made, one night, an ascent into heaven, an event still celebrated in the Muslim religious calendar. In Medina, the Prophet included as a part of his prophetic role his responsibilities as the political and military leader.

The rise and spread of Islam validates the Prophet's message for the Muslim. With the certitude provided by history and by the Qur'an, Muslims repeat, "I bear witness that there is no God but God and that Muhammad is his apostle," affirming both the centrality of God and the importance of Muhammad as the bearer of divine revelation, which is the role of the true prophet. That Muhammad could not read or write, and was as human as any other human being, serves only to emphasize for the Muslim the divine origin of the revelation itself. That Muhammad's prophethood led him to be not only a religious leader but also a military and political leader points to the scope of the prophetic task within the providential election anᵣ guidance of God.

The Community of Islam

The unity which has its origin in God, which is lived in obedience to the Qur'an, and which is the culmination of that work initiated through the Prophet, bears its fruit in the creation of the community of Islam, the *ummah*. The Islamic understanding of community needs special attention in light of contemporary events. Those who do Islam are united in the community of the faithful. This community must bear the responsibility for the success or failure of the Islamic witness. For Muslims, the health and welfare of that community is a very serious matter.

How is the well-being of the community sustained? Though ultimately everything proceeds from the grace of God, nevertheless the merciful God has indicated that certain things are to be believed and certain other things are to be practiced. The beliefs have been discussed in previous pages. The religious practices need some interpretation, because it is in the performance of ritual that the unity of the community finds its outward expression.

The obligatory practices of Islam are known as the Five Pillars of Islam. All of them are acts of worship; Muslims everywhere, with some minor variations, perform them in the same way.

The most important ritual is the recitation of the phrase, "I bear witness that there is no God but God and that Muhammad is his apostle." Though strictly speaking Islam has no creed, this statement is the universal declaration of Islamic belief. Called the Shahadah (that is, "the bearing of witness"), when uttered it frees the mind and heart of the believer to be loyal only to God and to be obedient to the divine guidance revealed through the Prophet.

The second pillar is that of prayer, specified by the term *salat,* which means "worship." Prayer is therefore, in its essence, worship. Muslims are to pray each day according to a prescribed pattern and at five prescribed times: at dawn, at midday, in the afternoon, at sunset, and at night. The recitation of these prayers does not automatically bring God's favor, for the intent of the heart and mind and the condition of the body must be pure, devoid of self-interest and indifference, and uncontaminated by the world. One must prepare for prayer by both a spiritual and a physical washing so that God alone may be praised. Prayer in Islam is not just a mental and verbal activity. Because the whole person must praise God, Muslim prayer includes physical activity such as requiring various body postures at specified places in the prayer ritual. Passages from the Qur'an are included in prayer so that one's dependence upon the divine guidance is not set aside by concerns imposed by the world. Because the prayer cycle begins before sunrise and concludes after sunset, worshipers are enabled to remember throughout the whole day that they are servants of God, dependent in every way upon God's daily sustenance. It is good for these prayers to be performed in the mosque, the place of prayer. Generally they are performed wherever worshipers find themselves when the prescribed time is at hand. The noon prayer on Friday should, however, be performed in the mosque. The person who leads prayer at the mosque is called the *imam.* Along with *salat,* Muslims are encouraged to perform *dua,* nonobligatory prayers of a more spontaneous nature. God may thus be entreated to respond to the special needs and concerns of the believer and the community. Whether obligatory or voluntary, all prayers are offered facing Mecca. Finally, in the act of prayer Muslims approach God directly. In Islam no mediator is postulated because no mediator is necessary. Mediation in Islamic understanding is a form of *shirk,* "idolatry."

The third pillar is *zakat* or "almsgiving." This act of worship reminds Muslims that they are but stewards of God, having oversight and responsibility for the preservation and well-being of all that has been entrusted to them. Those who have been blessed are called upon as stewards to bless those less fortunate than themselves. This is accomplished by taxing those who have made profit and distributing the tax to those who are in need. In this way are met the needs of the poor, the widowed, the orphaned, and the sick; and the stewards themselves are, in a sense, purified from the evils of greed and selfishness. Their stewardship is thus authenticated. The amount of tax that one must pay is determined by a complicated set of rules. Another set of regulations governs its distribution so that all is done fairly and justly, according to divine provision. As in the case of prayer, there is also a voluntary form of almsgiving called *sadaqah.* Muslims should always respond in this way to human need, thereby demonstrating a loyalty not only to their fellow human beings but also to God.

The most physically rigorous of the pillars is the fourth, *sawm,* "fasting." This takes place during the Muslim month of Ramadan, beginning at dawn and continuing until dark each day of the month. During the days in Ramadan, nothing may pass between the lips of the worshiper, and marital relations are suspended. By this ritual, Muslims demonstrate their dependence only upon God for that which is of worth and not upon the things of the world, even food or human pleasures. The daytime fast also emphasizes that the bounty of God should not be taken for granted, and that hardship in the name of God is preferable to worldly ease without God. The month, as a result, becomes one of intense devotion for many Muslims. Extra prayers are performed, acts of charity toward the poor are encouraged, and the entire Qur'an may be recited in special services of devotion. At the end of Ramadan is a celebration called the Id al-Fitr, "the feast of fast-breaking," one of the two most important Muslim festival days.

The fifth pillar is perhaps the one most familiar to outsiders. It is the Hajj, the pilgrimage to Mecca, that must be undertaken by every Muslim at least once in a lifetime. The wholeness of the individual believer and the wholeness of the community become indistinguishable in the performance of this act of worship. The unity of God nourishes the unity of the community as the acts of devotion performed by Abraham himself are reenacted and commemorated. The pilgrimage is undertaken during the first ten days of the month of Dhul Hijjah in the Muslim calendar. It closes with the celebration of the Id al-Adha, the festival of sacrifice, wherein each worshiper ritually sacrifices a sheep or goat just as Abraham sacrificed an animal in place of his son, Ishmael, in his time of testing. The Id al-Adha is the second important feast day in the Muslim calendar. As it is celebrated by those on the pilgrimage in Mecca, it is also celebrated by Muslims all over the world as they vicariously participate in the act of pilgrimage. While the details of the pilgrimage cannot be discussed here, their meaning and importance to Muslim devotion cannot be underestimated. By the pilgrimage the unity and continuity of the community in its devotion to God is acknowledged, witnessed to, and celebrated.

A large body of law provides for proper participation in these obligatory acts of worship. The community preserves its unity not only in the performance of the rituals but also in common obedience to an even larger body of law within which the rituals (pillars) are enshrined. This larger body of legal tradition is called the Shari'ah, the "way" or "right path." Taken as a whole, it is the complete embodiment of God's guidance for the community. The sources of the Shari'ah lie first of all in the Qur'an, then in the Sunnah of the Prophet, then in the application of the first two sources by analogy, and finally in the consensus of the community through the exercise of *ijtihad* (independent judgment). The collection and codification of the legal tradition took place during the first three centuries after the death of the Prophet. During that time, four major schools of jurisprudence developed. The differences between them are, however, not so great as to threaten the unity of the community. Because the whole matter of Islamic jurisprudence is complicated, we can deal here only with the importance of understanding the role of the Shari'ah in the life of the community.

Within Muslim life, the Shari'ah provides that divine guidance for all aspects of life which ensures that God's will is being obeyed. The Shari'ah defines for Muslims what faithfulness to God entails and the blessings that will result. To ignore, set aside, or abrogate the Shari'ah is thus to deny God. As was said at the beginning of this discussion, faithfulness or submission is not a matter of duty or obligation but rather a response to God's grace demonstrated in the provision of God's law. All the moral and ethical principles needed for wholesome community life, all aspects of the individual's own conduct within the community, are guided by the legal provisions of the Shari'ah. Obedience to these provisions ensures equality among all people and a just society. The unity of God is realized in the life of the community when the Shari'ah is obeyed. Further, these blessings are not just for Muslims only. They are available and essential to all human beings and their societies when they submit to the will of God.

Since the well-being of the community is dependent upon its obedience to Shari'ah, it is only natural that Muslims measure the well-being of their community against their faithfulness to the Shari'ah. Therefore it is the obligation of Muslim governments to see that a Muslim nation rules itself by the Shari'ah law. Where Muslims are not in control of political structures, the community must maintain for itself the obedience that is required. A concern for political structures and their importance is derived from the all-embracing character of the Shari'ah. Since all of life is a service to the will of God, there can be no separation between religion and state, to use the rhetoric that characterizes Western political thought. Every aspect of life, whether personal, social, communal, political, religious, economic, or cultural, is encompassed and integrated within the Shari'ah. In this way human life maintains balance and harmony, because each aspect receives its just due as God has commanded and contributes its share to the well-being of the whole.

Not only are Muslims obliged to seek the enactment of the Shari'ah as the means by which the welfare of the community is maintained and success in this life is achieved, they must also take seriously any person, state, program, or initiative that threatens to usurp the prerogatives of the Shari'ah. The community is promised success now. When the community fails, Muslims must undertake those activities which will reverse the failure. In this respect the prophetic model and the pattern of community life under the first rulers or caliphs (the Arabic term is *khalifah*, "successor") after the Prophet are normative for the modern community. Several activities are thus enjoined upon the community. The first is *jihad*, "struggle" or "effort" on behalf of God. The greater *jihad* is the internal struggle against evil, temptation, and idolatry in which all believers are engaged. The lesser *jihad* is the defensive action that the community must pursue when it is attacked from without. Some Muslim organizations are involved in what is called *da'wah*, "the call to be obedient to God" or "missionary activity," in an effort to preserve and strengthen the community against pressures from the outside. Mainly this activity is directed toward establishing those programs and institutions that will nurture the believers, particularly when they must live in a secular society. But the effort at *da'wah* may also be directed toward those who stand outside the community.

There are many other provisions of the Shari'ah that are important but cannot be discussed here. Taken together, they are accepted as the manifestation of God's compassionate love for creation and a means by which the unity of God is realized in the unity of all human life. This is the ideal. In actuality, the community is divided in various ways, each division seeking, within the broader content of the Shari'ah, to be obedient to the divine guidance. The major division in the community is between the Sunni and Shi'ah Muslims. The former take their name from the word *sunnah*, which means "path" and refers to the path of tradition. The Sunni are the ones who adhere to tradition. This group constitutes about 90 percent of the total Muslim community. The second group derives its name from the historical circumstances that led to the division. At the death of the Prophet, a group of people thought that Ali, the cousin and son-in-law of Muhammad, and Ali's descendants should be the caliphs of the community. Ali became the fourth caliph. When his second son, Hussain, was martyred in the battle of Kerbala (a city in Iraq) and could not succeed him, the *shi'ati Ali* ("party of Ali" or "followers of Ali") dissociated itself from the main body of Muslims, which it had opposed. After that break, certain doctrinal differences also developed, the most distinctive being that of the Imamate, wherein those spiritual leaders that are called Imams by the Shi'ah community were understood to have been a continuing source of the divine law, an understanding of the role of the imam that is heresy from the Sunni point of view. Apart from these doctrinal differences, Shi'ahs adhere in general to the Shari'ah. Today Shi'ahs live mainly in Iran, Lebanon, and Iraq.

Though it hardly represents a division within the community, the Sufi movement (*suf,* "wool," a reference to the woolen clothing worn) is worthy of note. The Sufis are Islamic mystics, those who not only seek to follow the Shari'ah but also desire to pattern their lives after the spirituality of the Prophet. Each Sufi generally belongs to a particular school or order oriented around the teachings of a Sufi leader or guide. Each order defines for itself the mystical "path" or "way" that one must follow in order to be united with God. The Sufi movement is known to the Western world primarily through the beautiful poetry that several outstanding Sufis have produced.

The call to submit to God has been answered, as evidenced in the growth and spread of Islam throughout the whole world. There are today almost nine hundred million Muslims. Like the adherents of every other religious community and tradition, Muslims on occasion will fail to live up to their ideals or will use religious ideals to achieve selfish ends. In either case they are unfaithful to Islam. Religious claims, when judged true, have the characteristic of spreading beyond the failures or successes of one generation of believers to appeal afresh to later generations. Such has been the case with Islam. Therefore its faith and practice must be taken seriously by all who in their own way have responded to the divine call to faithfulness. Anything less would be a denial of God. This brief outline is a first step toward that greater understanding.

2

Christian—Muslim Relations:
A Historical Overview

History is important to Muslims and to Christians, not only because the beginnings and development of these two faith communities are clearly historical facts but also because each takes seriously a belief that God continually interacts with humanity in everyday events and relationships. This history of their relations impacts current realities perhaps more powerfully than do their visions of the future. Having a shared history means that attitudes toward and impressions of each other tend to color all attempts to change or improve relationships. This chapter looks briefly at some of the major historical events involving Christians and Muslims. These events illustrate the development of important attitudes of each faith community toward the other that influence relationships today.

After the Roman emperor Constantine embraced the Christian faith (A.D. 312), the relationship of church and state changed dramatically. After more than two centuries of persecution, Christians found themselves involved in affairs of state, with results that persist to the present. In addition to creating church-state dilemmas, Constantine built the new capital at Constantinople (now Istanbul), beginning a process that ultimately divided the Holy Roman Empire into eastern and western sections. The division between East and West was reflected in the decisions of the early ecumenical councils. One such

---

This chapter is an edited and amended version of a condensation by Lawrence H. Richards of a longer paper on the same subject, also written by him.

assembly was the Council of Chalcedon in 451. The issue there centered on the theological formulation of the nature of Christ. The council rejected the monophysite formulation (Christ was only and wholly divine) of the Coptic (Egyptian), Armenian (Gregorian), and Syrian (Jacobite) Orthodox churches in the East in favor of the two-nature formulation (Christ is one person, truly divine and truly human) of the Greek Orthodox and Latin churches. Controversies such as these and power struggles within the church weakened the Christian community. When Muslim rule was established, for many the disunity of the church made the Christian faith a less acceptable alternative when compared to Islam.

The Early History of Relationships

The first Christians to know any Muslims, and thus to form any relations or set any patterns of behavior with them, were the few living in Mecca, Medina, and the surrounding central areas of the Arabian peninsula in the early decade of the seventh century. Two Christian centers were Najran in the southwest (North Yemen today) and al-Hirah, west of the Euphrates River (Iraq today). These Christians were of the Syrian Orthodox (Jacobite) and Nestorian churches, as were most of the several Christian Arab tribes, such as the Beni Hanifa and Beni Taghlib. They surrendered to Muhammad and either paid tribute (and remained Christian) or converted to Islam. The third choice, to wage war with the Muslim armies, was chosen by only a few, and without success.

Comparatively little is known of the influence these Christian contemporaries of Muhammad had on him. It appears that Muhammad may have had contacts with Christian monks while traveling as a merchant between Arabia and Damascus. He was supported in believing and proclaiming his early revelations by his wife, Khadijah, and her Christian cousin, Waraqah. Certain of his followers went to Abyssinia in 615 to avoid persecution. There the king of Abyssinia, a Christian, welcomed them as fellow believers in God. During his last ten years, Muhammad functioned as statesman and political leader as well as prophet. In this period Christians living under the Prophet's rule were granted protection and recognized as People of the Book, as believers in the same God who was revealed through the holy books. This protected status for Christians (and Jews) has remained a part of the Shari'ah.

After Muhammad's death in 632, his successors quickly gained control of the Arabian peninsula and then moved into the "fertile crescent" regions of Iraq, Persia, Anatolia, Syria, and Egypt. The Greek Byzantines were pushed back, with many of the (non-Chalcedonian) Christian population accepting life under their new conquerors as offering a better standard of justice and rule than the "state of oppression and tyranny" under which they had been living. Many of the monophysite writers from the seventh century saw the rise of Islam as a sign of God's anger and judgment against the sins of the Chalcedonian Orthodox establishment.

The perspective from Constantinople was quite different, however, and the fall of Jerusalem to Muslim armies in 636 marked the beginning of a new epoch, leading eventually to efforts by European Christians to regain access to the "holy places" in the medieval Crusades four and a half centuries later. From the first, however, the Muslims treated the Christians and Jews in Jerusalem like people in other places they captured. Those who surrendered and agreed to pay the tribute demanded were allowed to practice their faith and were protected according to Muslim law. This continued a custom developed by the Sassanid Persians in dealing with their religious minority groups in earlier centuries. The option was always open for individuals or groups to convert to Islam, although as Muslims they had less status for many years than the original Arab conquerors. Tolerance, but with defined levels of social status, generally marked the Muslim rule.

In the expansion of Muslim rule during this early period, Muslim conquerors occupied Spain and invaded southern France. Their northward advance was halted by Charles Martel at the Battle of Tours in 732. From the Muslim point of view, this was not a major engagement. Christian historians have represented it as a turning point in the fortunes of the invading Muslim armies. In fact, its greatest significance lies in the use of this event by medieval Christians to justify their attitudes against Islam.

The earliest center of Muslim power to develop outside of Mecca was the city of Damascus, where the Umayyad dynasty began to rule about 661. Christians in that region had adjusted fairly quickly to their new rulers, and Syrian Christians (Jacobites) formed the bulk of Caliph Mu'awiyah's army. The financial controller of the former Byzantine government, Mansur ibn Sarjun, continued to serve the new government, as did many other Christians from the several churches.

Mansur's grandson, John, grew up playing with the caliph's son, Yazid. Later John became the Bishop of Damascus. His approach to Islam reflects the influence Christians exerted on the early Muslims, particularly in transferring Greek rational philosophies to the emerging Islamic culture.

John of Damascus is best known, however, as the author of *Dialogue Between a Saracen and a Christian,* a treatise written as a manual of dialectics and apologetics for eighth-century Christians. His objective was to provide a model to enable Christians to understand the views and methods of Muslims, whom he considered to be heretics, and to equip Christians to argue with their conquerors. The *Dialogue* appears to have been a literary device rather than a record of an actual dialogue, but the issues raised between the two sides are of real concern to both Christians and Muslims, and the debate often continues today with little change from the questions and answers, charges and responses, that John outlined twelve centuries ago.

The interchange of culture and ideas that began in Damascus in the seventh century continued throughout the following three centuries, during which the Abbasids ruled most of the Muslim world from Baghdad. In this Golden Age of Islamic civilization, translations into Arabic were made of the philosophic works of Aristotle, the works of Plato and the neo-Platonists, and most of Galen's medical writings, as well as of many Persian and Indian scientific treatises. Christians did much of the translation work, particularly from Greek, and served society as physicians and financial administrators. Gradually the development of Muslim religious and communal institutions attracted converts from the various religious communities, and Christians slowly lost status. The Nestorian patriarch had a privileged residence in the new capital of Islam, while the Jacobites were denied direct access to the caliphs. During the eighth and ninth centuries, Nestorian missionaries traveled extensively throughout Asia, placing bishops in Afghanistan, Tibet, India, China, and several of the Central and Southeast Asian regions.

By the mid-eleventh century, Seljuk Turks had moved from central Asia to Baghdad, and Tughril Beg was installed as the first sultan (regent) of the Abbasids in 1056. As he and his successors strengthened and reunited the far-flung empire, Christians were replaced by Turks in the mercenary army and many other positions. Islamization proceeded more quickly, and Seljuks began to be so successful in advancing against the Byzantines in Anatolia that the Byzantine emperor asked for European military aid. The responses by Crusaders established one pattern of harsh militant relationships that still colors attitudes between Christians and Muslims.

Many significant theological developments took place during the time of the Abbasids. Sufi mysticism spread in all directions from the Fertile Crescent. Several schools of Islamic theology developed around Baghdad. Two of these schools were the Mu'tazilites and the Sunni Ash'arites, who differed markedly over their understanding of the divine attributes. The latter's founder, al-Ashari, developed dialectical theology *(kalam)* as an accepted formulation of Islamic doctrines.

This kind of intellectual development was indicative of the great heights Muslim civilization had reached at a time when Europe was in the Dark Ages. Muslim scholarship and knowledge were transmitted to Europe through North Africa and Spain by means of the works of people like Avicenna (Ibn Sina; 980–1037) and Averroës (Ibn Rushd; 1126–1198). Western mathematics and medicine, even the Enlightenment itself, were made possible by the accomplishments of Muslim scholars.

The Crusades

The definitive event that influenced the primary attitudes of most Westerners toward Islam was the series of Crusades launched from Europe at the end of the eleventh century to recapture the "holy land." Following an appeal by Pope Urban II in 1095, the first wave of armies took Jerusalem four years later and continued to pass through Asia Minor into the lands of the eastern Mediterranean for the next two centuries.

The exploits of the crusading knights have been given many romantic and heroic embellishments in Western popular thought. Among Eastern Christians and Muslims, however, there remains to the present time a legacy of bitterness, alienation, and suspicion because of the havoc and destruction the Crusaders caused. The motives that generated these militaristic adventures were complex. They included rivalries between various commercial interests, particularly Venice and Genoa, similar rivalries between emerging nation-states of Europe, and the desire of the Roman papacy to reunite all Christendom under its banner.

In addition, the Crusades were the first major response by Europeans, who were by then largely Christian, to the Islamic invasions of the seventh and eighth centuries. The Christian resentment against Muslim control of the holy places in Jerusalem became the motivation for Christian participation in the Crusades.

Many permanent results have come from the Crusades. Steven Runciman states that

> the Crusades form a central fact in medieval history. Before their inception the centre of our civilization was placed in Byzantium and in the lands of the Arab Caliphate. Before they faded out the hegemony in civilization had passed to western Europe. Out of this transference modern history was born.[*]

In this process, as the Crusaders fought the Byzantines and briefly established their own government in Constantinople, the schism between Eastern and Western Christianity became

---

[*]Steven Runciman, *A History of the Crusades,* 3 vols. (Cambridge University Press, 1951), vol. 1, p. xi.

complete. Christians in the Middle East were weakened by the
Crusades and even today remain suspect in the eyes of their
Muslim neighbors as at least potential agents of "Western"
civilization and religion. Their witness to the gospel of Jesus
Christ in its central themes of love and peace were made in-
credible by the actions of militant Crusaders.

> The chief permanent effect of the Crusades in the Near East was
> in trade. Colonies of Western merchants had flourished in the
> Levant ports under crusading rule. They survived under the
> Muslim reconquest and developed a considerable trade both of
> export and import. In 1183 Saladin, writing to the Caliph in
> Baghdad, justified his encouragement of this trade in these
> words: "This constitutes an advantage for Islam and an injury for
> Christianity." The thunder of the church in Europe against this
> trade and the decrees of excommunication against those who
> engaged in it were ineffective.*

In contrast to the Crusaders, one of the leaders of the medieval church who sought to encourage dialogue and understanding by Christians instead of confrontations with Muslims was
the energetic Abbot of Cluny, Peter the Venerable (1094–
1157), who administered "a monastic empire comprising
some ten thousand monks in more than six hundred mon-
asteries located throughout western Christendom."† Dis-
tressed by the outrageous lies and vilification about Muhammad and the Muslims that were circulating in Europe under the
stimulus of the Crusades, Peter resolved to address the common ignorance about Islam by commissioning a study project
in Toledo, Spain, to translate the Qur'an and Islamic traditions,
as well as some of the standard Arab Christian apologetic
works.

Peter was convinced that the Crusades were leaving out the
most important goal for Christians, the conversion of Muslims,
and thus concluded his study project with a clear handbook on

---

*Bernard Lewis, *The Arabs in History* (New York: Harper & Brothers,
1960), p. 153.

†James Kritzeck, *Peter the Venerable and Islam* (Princeton: Princeton University Press, 1964), p. 4.

Islamic beliefs, with apologetic comments, and with a long article directed to Muslims. "I attack you," he wrote, "not as some often do, by arms, but by words; not with force, but with reason, not with hatred, but in love. . . . I love; loving, I write to you; writing, I invite you to salvation."*

Peter's collection of translations from Arabic into Latin and his understanding of Islamic beliefs influenced Europeans' understanding of Islam for nearly five hundred years, particularly when Luther and Melanchthon, in 1543, wrote introductions to the publication of these translations of the Qur'an and other Islamic works. Other European scholars also engaged in the medieval attempts at understanding Islam, such as Raymond Lull in the latter part of the thirteenth century.

Unfortunately this attitude was seen only in a minority of people at that time. The contrary approach was common and is evidenced in one of the most notorious of events in the history of the Christian church, the institution of the Inquisition by Gregory IX (1227–1241) to combat heresy. In Spain, under Ferdinand and Isabella (1499), it led to forced conversion and/or expulsion of Muslims and Jews from Spain. The final order for deportation in 1609 resulted in the forcible expulsion of all Muslims from Spanish soil. By the beginning of the seventeenth century, about three million Muslims had been either banished from Spain or executed by Christian leaders.

During the period of the Crusades, a confederation of nomadic tribes from Mongolia swept across China, northern India, Russia, and eastern Prussia into Europe, and through Persia and the Arab Fertile Crescent region to the borders of Egypt. Led by a succession of Khans, beginning with the famed Genghis Khan (1155–1227), this "horde" devastated most of the Islamic civilization. Inevitably the Mongols became involved in the politics of the Crusades and the rivalries between Christian and Muslim leaders. Eventually the Mongols became Muslim. Most Christian churches declined over the next cen-

---

*James Kritzeck, "Muslim-Christian Understanding in Medieval Times," *Comparative Studies in Society and History,* vol. 4 (1962), p. 395.

tury. By the time Timur-e-Lang reunited the Mongol Empire in 1369, the Christian church represented a small minority of the people.

The Ottoman Period

The theocracy called the Eastern Roman, or Byzantine, Empire represented independent Christianity to the majority of Muslims for the first seven Muslim centuries. Following the adventures of the Crusaders, the Greek Christians were gradually forced back into Europe from Asia Minor by the growing power of the Ottoman Empire. Beginning about 1300, a collection of warrior clans under the leadership of Osman resumed the traditional Islamic struggle against the "infidel" Byzantines and overran most of the Anatolian peninsula by 1340. They bypassed the capital, Constantinople, for about a century while pressing through the Balkans into Europe. By 1453, however, Mehmet II had conquered the city and realized an Islamic dream that had often been attempted. Greek Orthodox Christianity lost its long struggle to maintain its independent hegemony, and Sunni Islam gained a capital city, renamed Istanbul, which dominated the region until the early years of this century. This marked the beginning of the Ottoman Empire.

In the years immediately following, the Ottoman Turks expanded their control to the gates of Vienna and throughout the Arabic-speaking heartland of Islam to the borders of Persia, the Arabian peninsula, Egypt, and northern Africa. Conflicts with the Hapsburgs, Spain, Portugal, and the Italian city-states seriously threatened the Europeans and continued the Western popular view of Islam as a militant "movement of violence in the service of the Anti-Christ."* From the sixteenth century onward, Europeans generally saw Islam not as a theological problem but as a fearsome enemy. As the Ottoman Empire gradually disintegrated, it came to be discounted as "the sick

---

*Albert H. Hourani, *Europe and the Middle East* (Berkeley: University of California Press, 1980), p. 10.

man of Europe," fit only to be manipulated and dismembered.

When Constantinople fell to the Ottomans, ending the reign of the Byzantine emperor, many of his privileges and responsibilities were inherited by the Greek Orthodox Patriarch. He was made responsible to the Ottoman Sultan and became the head of the Christian *millet* (nation, community), in effect a caliph for all Christians under Ottoman rule. The Armenians arranged, eight years later, separate status for themselves and other non-Chalcedonian Christians. As the Ottomans enlarged their domain to include all the lands of the former Eastern Roman Empire, the Armenian Patriarch in Istanbul had final authority over the Monophysite Copts of Egypt, the Jacobite Syrian Orthodox, the Nestorians in Mesopotamia, the Maronite Catholics, and others. The "Ecumenical Patriarch" of Constantinople gained jurisdiction over the "Melkite" Greek Orthodox of Antioch, Jerusalem, and Alexandria. This was an attempt by the Ottomans to bring uniformity into what had already evolved, through the experience of these several *millet* communities since the seventh century, into complex, distinct, and often competing legal systems governing all personal and social affairs of the Christians within each community. Jews were similarly accorded millet status by the Ottomans within their empire, based on earlier Muslim practices with the *dhimmi*, minority communities who were granted a protected status under certain conditions.

The millet system continued in effect from the fifteenth century until the end of the Ottoman Empire in World War I. All the ancient churches eventually gained their own grants of autonomy as separate millets, particularly when Catholic Uniate churches related to Rome emerged during the sixteenth to eighteenth centuries from the various Eastern rite churches. A Protestant millet developed in the mid-nineteenth century as the result of the evangelical awakenings stimulated by Western missionaries.

The long-standing practice of separating peoples into communities by their religious identity has made participation by Christians in the modern nation-states somewhat difficult. Lebanon's attempt at achieving a balance between seventeen dif-

ferent millets in its national government has erupted in civil
war in recent years. Similar dynamics are also at work within
the Palestinian–Israeli situation.

Protestant Missions in the Colonial Period

The earliest Reformers, such as Calvin and Knox, concen-
trated their attention primarily on the evangelization of the
Roman church in Europe and did not consider mission to the
other parts of the world as essential. Knox's worldview was
probably typical of Protestants in his time: "What is Asia?
Ignorance of God. What is Africa? Abnegation of the verie
Savior, our Lord Jesus. What is in the churches of the Gre-
cianis? Mahomet and his false sect. What is in Rome? The
greatest ydoll of all others, that man of Syn!"*

Protestants and Catholics from Europe, however, did travel
throughout the world as merchants and soldiers, as well as
missionaries, during the years of exploration and colonization.
As Europeans explored alternative routes to the spices and silks
of India and Asia, they bypassed the costly overland commerce
controlled by Muslims, by developing seaports along the coasts
of Africa, India, and Southeast Asia, as well as those of North
and South America. As northern European states (mostly Protestant) gradually overtook Spain and Portugal (mostly Catholic) in these pursuits, economic and other strategic interests
superseded the religious imperatives, but a mixture of motives
continues to the present day.

Although a few pioneering Protestant missionaries reached
India and other regions from Europe in the eighteenth century, the major growth of modern missions took place in the
early years of the nineteenth. Sparked by evangelical revivals,
mission "stations" were established in most places where, not
just coincidentally, merchants, colonial administrators, and
educators from "Western" countries were also found. Attitudes toward Hindus, "pagans," and other non-Muslim peo-

---

*John Knox, "Godly Letter to the Faithful in London, A. D. 1554," cited
by E. C. Dewick, *The Christian Attitude to Other Religions* (Cambridge University Press, 1953), pp. 116–117.

ples were often more congenial than those directed toward the Muslims of Africa and Asia. Non-Muslims were viewed as potential or actual allies who were likely to be more responsive to the calls for conversion by these early missionaries.

Much effort was expended on apologetics, the mixture of pietism, rationalism, and medieval polemics that marked nineteenth-century disputations by Christians and Muslims. One key person was a German, Karl G. Pfander, who went to India to work with the Church Missionary Society. He translated into Urdu his first book on Islam and Christianity, *Mizan al-Haqq* (Balance of Truth), which he had written earlier during his travels among Muslims and Armenians in Georgia and Persia. Muslims in northwestern India felt threatened by his linguistic abilities in Arabic, Persian, and Urdu, as well as by his direct comparisons of the "truth" of Christianity with what he claimed to be the "falsity" of Islam. By 1852 a Muslim scholar, Maulana Rahmat Allah Kairanawi, published a refutation of Pfander's work, the *Izhar al-Haqq* (Revelation of Truth) and led the Muslim *ulama* (scholars) in resisting Christian activities. In a public debate a couple of years later, Rahmat Allah used newly developed European biblical criticism to refute the fundamentalist missionaries and substantiate Muslim claims that the Qur'an abrogates the Bible, as well as to demonstrate that Christians corrupt the scriptures and misunderstand God as Trinity. Both books are still being reprinted and circulated as examples of Christian and Muslim apologetics.

Other approaches of Christian missionaries included establishing educational institutions and health-care centers such as hospitals and clinics. American Presbyterians participated in these activities along with Europeans, particularly Anglicans and Scots Presbyterians. They emphasized the development of indigenous churches to take over and operate these service programs. The members of these indigenous churches, for the most part, did not come from the conversions of Muslims. Rather they came from other Christian churches or non-Muslim groups. Thus the issues of church unity and ecumenism also gradually became important to mission policy.

The impact of Europeans on the world of Islam was most keenly felt in the nineteenth century and the first half of the twentieth, when over a dozen Western nations scrambled for power in those parts of Asia, Africa, and Europe where Islam was predominant.

Western colonial domination placed enormous stress on the Muslims. For centuries Muslims had faced many challenges, from Crusaders to Mongols, but nothing had challenged the core of Islamic life as seriously as the sweep of Western civilization brought by the new conquerors. Conservative Islam, the traditional pattern of life set by the Shari'ah, and the medieval synthesis of Islamic culture were forced to meet the twentieth-century world from a new position of defeat and subjugation. The choices for Muslims were difficult. They could emphasize the fundamental principles and practices of Islam, involving themselves in the rest of the world only as much as the tradition allowed; adopt a secular approach and emulate the victorious Europeans; or reform Islam so as to reconcile it with the rest of the world, particularly Western civilization, Christian or otherwise.

The Situation Today

Politically, the reaction in most areas to the dominion by the imperial powers of the recent past was a struggle to throw off Western domination and to create independent nation-states after World War II. The internal struggle continues in most cases, with Muslims arguing vigorously among themselves for one of the basic choices already noted. With few exceptions, however, the political independence of each state seems reasonably secure. The issues of economic and social interdependence remain highly volatile, because the value systems and the legal and ethical questions of the modern era defy simple or traditional responses. Rejecting the West emotionally while continuing to depend on the West economically seems to be the condition of many Muslims today.

These issues have produced a revival or resurgence within the Muslim community. (See chapter 3, p. 61, for a fuller discussion of Islamic revivalism.) One aspect of this revival has been that Muslim nations are seeking to clarify what Islam means as related to modern national identity. Often the process has been accompanied by revolution, as different groups have sought to impose their particular understandings on the nation. The case studies given in chapter 4 illustrate how the revivalist movement affects Muslim nations.

Of crucial importance for understanding the contemporary Muslim world is the situation in the Middle East created by the Palestinian–Israeli conflict. The creation of the state of Israel in 1948 accompanied by the displacement of the Palestinian people from their traditional homeland has had a profound effect upon Christian–Muslim relations everywhere. The Zionist dream of a "national homeland" in Palestine for Jewish people was supported by many in the West as an appropriate alternative after the Nazi holocaust. To the Muslim world, however, the creation of the state of Israel was seen as a direct challenge in its heartland, with the control of the holy city of Jerusalem a major issue. Muslims are aware of Israel's military successes. To be faithful to Islam, they feel that they must reverse these successes by a struggle to redeem what they understand to be the injustice committed against the Palestinian people. Israelis see the contemporary situation of their own nation as a minority community in the Arab world as the continuation of a historical problem: "The problems of minorities that are denied their rights are transferred to the national plane; the national sovereignty of a *Dhimmi* State is denied."*

Arab Christians, many of whom are Palestinians, often feel caught in the middle of conflicting ideologies as well as in actual warfare. They shared with the Jews a long-standing official *dhimmi* (protected) status under their Arab Muslim conquerors, and they yearn for similar equitable arrangements within modern societies. At the same time, their national and cultural identities as Arabs often lead them to stand vigorously against what they see as the injustices that have accompanied the occupation of the land of Palestine by Jewish refugees. The ambiguity of their position makes the Arab Christian community extremely vulnerable to conflicting ideologies.

---

*Bat Ye'or, *The Dhimmi: Jews and Christians Under Islam* (Madison, N.J.: Fairleigh Dickinson University Press, 1985), p. 156.

Mission and Relations

Dr. Khurshid Ahmad, Co-Convener of the 1976 international consultation of Muslims and Christians held in Chambésy, Switzerland, on "Christian Mission and Islamic Da'wah," has said that "the role of Christian missions in the Muslim world is regarded by the Muslims to be at the root of estrangement between the Christian and Muslim worlds."* No history of the relations between Muslims and Christians would be complete, therefore, without attention to the increased missionary activities of Christians in all parts of the world in the past two centuries, as well as more recent similar activities of Muslims. Mission or witness has always been a primary activity of the Christian community, but other concerns for the survival and maintenance of the church have often given the impression that witness and outreach to others was the task of certain "specialists" (evangelists).

In response to the periodic revivals and spiritual awakenings in eighteenth- and nineteenth-century Europe and North America, various agencies were organized, such as the American Board of Commissioners for Foreign Missions (established in 1810) and such denominational agencies as the Board of Foreign Missions of the Presbyterian Church in the U.S.A. (established in 1837) to engage in missions in many areas of the globe. From the beginning, Presbyterians have seen mission as the work done primarily by organized churches throughout the world in partnership with one another.

Since World War II, the reality of autonomous Christian churches existing in nearly every nation on earth was brought into focus through the formation of the World Council of Churches and of regional and national councils of churches. The ecumenical movement built upon the relationships that missions had created in earlier times. Colonial dependency was replaced by freedom and its corresponding responsibilities.

This development within the Christian churches, imperfect and incomplete though it remains, has been paralleled to some extent within the Muslim community. Every year more and

---

*International Review of Mission, vol. 65, no. 260 (1976), p. 367.

more Muslims are enabled by means of the support provided by their governments to go on the Hajj. There they experience the universal and international character of the Muslim community. In addition, there are several international Muslim organizations that cross political and other boundaries to enlarge the Islamic sense of unity and cooperation. The Muslim World League is one example.

The ecumenical movement within the Christian community not only affected Christian churches but sought also to explore new directions for the relationships between Christians and people of other religious traditions. The World Council of Churches established its Office for Dialogue with People of Living Faiths to study and promote better understanding and relations. Dialogue was seen as the chief means to achieve this. As a result, the World Council of Churches held many conferences and interfaith meetings all over the world for Christian–Muslim dialogue. The Roman Catholic Church has also been involved in interfaith activity. It has established a Secretariat for Non-Christians in Rome for the promotion of dialogue between Christians and others. The *Nostra Aetate* statement of Vatican II (Declaration on the Relation of the Church to Non-Christian Religions; 1965) is a major theological contribution to interfaith concerns. The efforts of these international organizations provide hope for the future of Christian–Muslim relations.

There are still many gaps to bridge between Christians and Muslims. Many individuals and groups have sought to understand the "other" through dialogue in its various forms. Councils of churches have established offices to facilitate such activities. Only determined efforts, carried through with effective and sustained support on a worldwide scope, intending to address the many theological and social issues that have separated Muslims and Christians, can be expected to make significant headway in enhancing cooperation and achieving reconciliation. This is essentially one of *the* major mission tasks for the immediate future.

What can be learned from this rapid survey of over fourteen centuries of interaction between the two largest religiously defined groups of human beings on the planet? Are the differences essential, or are they primarily accidents of history that can be resolved? The theological issues are fundamental and challenging, requiring creativity in finding new approaches that avoid the old charges of heresy, falsification of revelation, and unfaithfulness in communal and individual lives. The most fundamental of these issues are discussed in chapter 5.

Of immediate concern for many Christians, particularly those living as minorities where Muslims predominate, are the issues of human and civil rights, including equal access to social, political, and economic opportunities and participation in all levels of life. The traditional law of the Shari'ah seems in some ways to discriminate against non-Muslims. Adequate forms of redress and justice seem to be a high priority in certain places. The volatility of this matter can be seen vividly in the Lebanon and Palestinian–Israeli conflicts. The varied experience of many newly independent countries, such as Nigeria, Egypt, Sudan, Syria, Pakistan, and Indonesia, might be analyzed with profit and shared in international forums working on the peaceable development of peoples.

Highly desirable also would be attempts to develop one-world consciousness among all peoples. Important social and political differences do exist, but they need to be dealt with carefully from a global perspective.

Adequate methods need to be devised to deal with the alienating episodes of the past, the "sins of omission and commission" in our common history. A sense of guilt for the Crusades is not a strong factor for most Westerners, but anger and shame about those events are still strong in many Muslims, especially Middle Easterners. The exploitations and cruelties perpetrated by the imperialists need adequate restitution. Since it is manifestly impossible for anyone to go back in time and change whatever happened, it is important that there be developed processes whereby people with historic grievances can seek and find forgiveness and, through reconciliation, forget the hurts and move toward wholeness and fruitful lives.

3

The Contemporary Muslim World: An Overall Profile

This chapter aims at drawing a brief yet faithful portrait of the Islamic world today. The demographic, ethnocultural, socio-economic, and political dimensions will be presented in a way that attempts to make clear both the unity and the variety that characterize the world of Islam, as well as the dynamics currently at work in it. While these various aspects are treated separately, for purposes of description and analysis, they are not in fact separate from each other. This is most clear in the final section, which deals with Islamic revivalism or resurgence.

A Demographic Profile

It seems appropriate to begin with the people who call themselves Muslims. Who are they? Where are they found? How numerous are they?

The attempt to show the location and enumeration of Muslims first takes the form of as accurate a summary as possible, in Table 1, of the numbers and percentage of Muslims in the various regions of the world. The numbers and percentage of Christians are given also for comparative purposes. The figures given, however, are estimates only. While they are as accurate as possible, the margin of error could be several percentage

---

This chapter is a condensation by Frank L. Cooley of his longer paper on the same subject.

Table 1. Muslims and Christians in the World (Estimated, 1985)

RELIGION	POPULATION	MUSLIMS			CHRISTIANS		
		Number	% of population	% of all Muslims	Number	% of population	% of all Christians
The Middle East	151,490,000	143,468,000	94.70	16.04	3,991,000	2.63	0.30
North Africa	103,900,000	97,085,000	93.44	10.35	5,175,000	5.00	0.35
South Asia	1,003,800,000	284,492,000	28.34	31.80	33,460,000	3.40	2.24
East & Central Asia & U.S.S.R.	1,522,579,000	63,644,000	4.28	7.11	122,278,000	8.00	8.17
Mainland South-east Asia	158,585,000	3,840,000	2.42	0.43	7,090,000	4.50	0.47
Insular South-east Asia & Oceania	262,896,000	158,496,000	60.29	17.71	87,010,000	33.10	5.81
Sahelian Tier of African Countries	91,650,000	56,222,000	61.30	6.22	24,200,000	26.60	1.62

Region							
Southern Africa	345,257,000	71,576,000	20.73	8.00	187,509,000	54.31	12.53
Eastern Europe	162,912,000	7,739,000	4.75	0.87	127,771,000	78.43	7.86
Western Europe	326,097,000	5,348,000	1.64	0.60	286,622,000	87.89	19.79
North America	265,066,000	3,157,000	1.19	0.26	234,043,000	88.30	15.63
Caribbean & Central America	136,374,000	200,000	.15	0.02	126,777,000	93.00	8.47
South America	265,309,000	811,000	.30	0.09	251,091,000	94.60	16.77
Totals	4,795,915,000	896,078,000	18.68	100.0	1,497,017,000	31.21	100.0

points up or down. Muslim sources, or those sympathetic to the Muslim community, were favored for figures on Muslims, and Christian sources for statistics on the Christian community. The map shows the distribution of Muslims in the world today. Some salient facts that emerge from a study of the demographic data on the Islamic world are summarized below.

In certain regions and countries the population is predominantly of one religion. There are 31 countries that are over 80 percent Muslim, and 54 countries that are over 80 percent Christian. Seven other countries are 50–79 percent Muslim; Christians constitute a similar proportion of the population in 20 countries.

While most of the world's Muslim and Christian countries are included in the above category, substantial numbers of Muslims and Christians live in societies where they are minorities. Muslims constitute 15 to 49 percent of the population in 19 countries and Christians make up similar percentages in 14 countries. Finally, in 22 countries Muslims and Christians each constitute 15 percent or less of the population.

Reflecting on the distribution and proportion of Muslims and Christians in the world, four observations seem to be in order.

First, neither Islam nor Christianity is present in substantial percentages in East and Central Asia, mainland Southeast Asia, or South Asia, except for Afghanistan, Pakistan, and Bangladesh, which are predominantly Muslim. Neither has made significant impact in those areas where the religions of Hinduism and Buddhism and the philosophical-cultural systems of Confucianism and Shintoism predominate.

Second, over the last several centuries, both Islam and Christianity have penetrated with marked success those areas where tribal religions have prevailed, and they continue to do so, most notably in sub-Saharan Africa.

Third, both Christian and Muslim faith communities have encountered opposition, constraints, and persecution in aggressively Marxist societies.

Fourth, of particular interest to those concerned with mission and *da'wah* and relations between the two faith communities, are those areas where both are active in significant num-

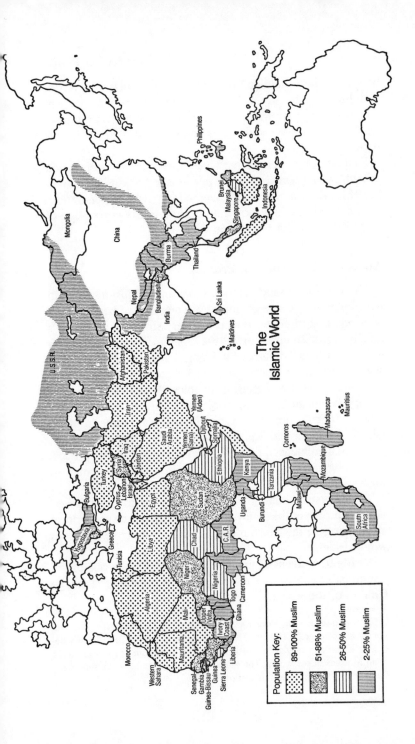

The Islamic World

Population Key:

89-100% Muslim

51-88% Muslim

26-50% Muslim

2-25% Muslim

bers but where neither predominates, particularly in Africa and India. Currently Lebanon, Egypt, the Sudan, and Indonesia—countries where Islam is the majority community—are being observed with lively interest and concern in this regard.

Demographic trends, particularly annual net population growth rates, point clearly to a percentage growth in the number of Muslims in the world, over at least the next generation, with a corresponding moderate decline in the percentage of Christians in world population.

An Ethnic Sociocultural Profile

The worship of God through Islam unites Muslims from all over the world in one community. The sense of being joined with other Muslims everywhere is very strong in a Muslim's life. In purely human terms, the Islamic community reflects unity within the diversity of ethnic, language, and cultural characteristics. In the case of ethnicity, there is a great mosaic of ethnic groups or "Muslim peoples,"* each with its own history, language, customs, mores, social structure, and values. These ethnic groups existed long before Islam came to them. Islamic faith and practice, the main source of Islamic culture, profoundly influenced their later development. In that process their indigenous culture became a part of and contributed to the variety evident in the Muslim world today.

To understand that world, it is necessary to identify and sketch a profile of the major groupings of language and culture areas that give the Muslim peoples their distinctive identities within Islam.

Nearly 91 percent of the world's Muslims speak one of the hundreds of subfamilies of five of the eight major language families of the world:

---

*This phrase is taken from Richard V. Weekes, *Muslim Peoples: A World Ethnographic Survey* (Westport, Conn.: Greenwood Press, 1984), which describes 190 ethnic and/or linguistic groups that constitute nearly 98 percent of all Muslims in the world. The introduction of this book is the source for the points summarized in this section.

- 340 million speak languages belonging to the Indo-Iranian (or Indo-Aryan) branch of the Indo-European family, such as Farsi (Persian), Baluchi, Kurdish, Pushtu, Sindhi, Urdu, Punjabi, and Bengali
- 170 million speak languages of the Afro-Asiatic family in Western Asia and North Africa, including Arabic, Somali, Hausa, and Berber
- 155 million speak languages in the Malayo-Polynesian family in Southeast Asia, including Malagasy, Malay, Indonesian, and Moro
- Nearly 100 million Muslims in Central Asia speak Turkic languages of the Ural-Altaic family, including Turks, Tartars, Uzbeks, Kazakhs, Uygur, and Kirghiz, among others
- Perhaps 50 million Muslims speak languages of the Niger-Congo family on the western side of Africa south of the Sahara, mainly Bantu, Wolof, Fulani, and Manding

Nine culture areas (geographic regions in which ethnic groups share significant culture commonalities), within which most Muslims live, have been identified (Weekes, pp. xxiv–xxv). They are:

1. The drylands of Southwest Asia, often called the Middle or Near East, the heartland of Arab culture
2. The lower Nile River delta, home of nearly 45 million Arabs who were once non-Arab Egyptians
3. The Mediterranean coast of North Africa, host of a culture composed of pre-Islamic Berber traditions overlaid by Arab cultures
4. The "sudan" ("black" in Arabic), a 1,000-mile-wide belt stretching from the Red Sea to the Atlantic Ocean, lying to the south of North Africa
5. The Northeast Ethiopic dry plains, forests, and sea coast, home of semi-sedentary peoples converted to Islam soon after its advent, including the Afar, Somali, Tigre, and Oromo.
6. The East African forested coast, with numerous trading cities occupied by culturally heterogeneous Arabs, Per-

sians, Indians, and Pakistanis intermarried with the native Bantu

7. The Central Asian steppes, dry highlands suitable to pastoral peoples, land of Turkmen, Tartars, Kazakhs, and Uzbeks, with the famous Muslim cities of Samarkand and Tashkent

8. The broad Aryan culture area stretching from Iran to Bangladesh, a land of mountains and plains adapted to pastoralism and sedentary farming

9. The Southeast Asian area of rivers, forests, peninsulas, and islands, whose peoples have developed a culture based on wet-rice farming, fishing, and seafaring.

Three basic patterns of living are found within these nine culture areas—nomadic, sedentary rural-based, and urban—with clearly evident overlapping and interaction between them. The socioeconomic culture patterns of these three lifestyles are distinct. The faithfulness with which people observe the practices of Islam may differ in each area, and especially between the 30 percent urban and 70 percent rural sectors of the population. The differences are particularly notable in the ways people live among and relate to their kin—primarily the degree to which, for example, the nuclear family, the joint or extended family, endogamous and exogamous marriage, and clan and tribal structures are evident in the three basic patterns of life.

A Socioeconomic Profile

Most Muslim peoples are part of the developing world—the "two thirds" world. They are still predominantly a rural people, living on land and under an economic system that returns very little to them for all their effort. The result is widespread poverty everywhere from the Atlantic coast of Africa to the Pacific coast of the Philippines and Indonesia. Those who are city dwellers generally share the frustrations of all nonindustrial urbanites: low income, high rates of unemployment and/or part-time employment, and crowded living conditions.

Yet their unfulfilled expectations are rising. Most of their countries have inherited a past of colonial subjugation and still remain largely dependent on and are the victims of economic, social, and political interests and systems dominated by either Western free enterprise or Eastern socialist powers. What results should not be surprising: violent responses in the form of actions by the victimized against those they perceive as their victimizers (Weekes, pp. xxi–xxii). This phenomenon will be treated in a later section.

Data for a more detailed view of the socioeconomic life of sixteen Muslim countries have been assembled in Table 2. All sixteen with the exception of Nigeria consider themselves to be Muslim countries. Five are in the Middle East, four in North Africa, three in South Asia, two in Insular Southeast Asia, and two in the Sahel region of Africa.

Though the figures are for 1980—except those for petroleum production, which are for 1982—the following tentative generalizations may be interesting and useful.

First, the largest Muslim populations (49.47 percent of all Muslims) are in South and Insular Southeast Asia, while those in the Middle East and North Africa, the heartland of Islam, constitute only 26.81 percent. In the latter countries, however, a higher percentage of the population is Muslim (94.4 percent, as over against a percentage of 81.1 in the former).

Second, the sixteen countries as a whole show a 2.9 percent annual net rate of population growth. For the Middle East countries, one of the world's most volatile regions, the net rate of increase is 3.4 percent. These unusually high growth rates have significant, if not ominous, economic as well as social and political implications for the future. (U.S. natural population growth is 0.7 percent per year.)

Third, life expectancy is still quite low—47 years in the South Asian and Sahelian Africa countries, and 54–55 years for the other countries. (Life expectancy in the United States is 74 years.)

Fourth, literacy rates also seem low, relatively speaking, ranging from 24 percent in South Asia to 73.5 percent for Insular Southeast Asia, with the Middle Eastern and Northern

Table 2. Socioeconomic Profile of Countries with a Muslim Population Over Seven Million

	Muslim population in millions	% of Mus-lims	Annual rate of population growth	Life expectancy in years	Per capita income in U.S. $	Industry as % of GNP	Agriculture as % of GNP	Education as % of GNP	Petroleum producing countries by % of total	Liter-acy rate %
MIDDLE EAST										
Iran	42.0	98	3.0	57.5	2,160	43	9	5.7	4.2 (5th)	47
Iraq	14.0	95	3.4	56.1	2,410	60	8	3.2	1.8 (14th)	43
Saudi Arabia	9.0	99	4.2	54.0	11,500	58	1	6.4	12.2 (3rd)	25
Syria	9.0	88	3.8	56.6	702	16	17	4.9		66
Turkey	49.5	99	2.5	53.7	1,300	26	22	3.6		60
mean	24.7	95.8	3.4	55.7	3,614	40.6	11.4	4.76		48.2
NORTH AFRICA										
Algeria	21.8	99	3.3	54.0	1,600	39	8	3.8	1.4 (16th)	42
Egypt	43.7	91	2.6	55.0	560	28	22	4.1		42
Morocco	22.7	99	3.2	53.0	800	25	18	6.0		71
Tunisia	7.0	99	2.5	55.0	1,200	21	14	6.4		47
mean	23.8	97	2.9	54.0	1,040	28.3	15.5	5.1		50.5

SOUTH ASIA										
Afghanistan	15.3	99	2.5	42.0	168	20	55	1.7		20
Bangladesh	86.3	85	2.8	47.0	105	7	53	1.5		29
Pakistan	92.2	97	2.8	52.0	280	18	27	2.0		23
mean	64.6	93.7	2.7	47.0	184	15	45	1.7		24
INSULAR S.E. ASIA										
Indonesia	145.0	88	2.3	50.0	415	36	26	2.0	2.5 (9th)	72
Malaysia	7.7	49	2.5	69.0	714	22	22	5.8		75
mean	76.4	68.5	2.4	59.5	564	29	24	3.9		73.5
SAHELIAN AFRICA										
Sudan	15.8	73	2.8	44.0	370	9	36	6.3		20
Nigeria	40.0	45	3.2	50.0	750	30	23	4.3	2.4 (10th)	34
mean	27.9	59	3.0	47.0	560	19.5	29.5	5.3		27
Totals: mean	38.8	87.7	2.96	53.1	1,565	28.6	22.6	4.2		46.3
Totals: median	22.3	96	2.90	53.9	732	25.5	22.0	4.2		42.5

African countries in between with 48.2 percent and 50.5 percent, and Sahelian Africa on the low side at 27 percent. (The rate is 88 percent in the United States.)

Fifth, the regions with highest per capita income (in U.S. dollars) were the Middle East ($3,614) and North Africa ($1,040), largely due to petroleum exports. The poorest region is South Asia, with no oil exports, at $184 per capita per year. The other countries are in between but on the low side. (U.S. per capita income is $10,580.)

Sixth, the Middle Eastern countries show up highest in size of the industrial sector of the economy, at 40.6 percent, largely due to petroleum production and refining. Sahelian Africa and South Asia were lowest, with 19.5 percent and 15 percent respectively. The mean figure for industry as a percentage of gross national product for all sixteen was 28.6 percent. (This figure was 22 percent for the United States.)

Seventh, as for the percentage of the agriculture sector in the economy, South Asian countries were highest (45 percent), yet surprisingly low in light of the fact that in all three, 75 percent of the population live from animal husbandry, fishing, and farming. (It is 2.9 percent for the United States.)

Finally, one relatively bright feature was the fact that these sixteen Muslim countries as a whole do not seem to be seriously lagging in their concern for education, with 4.2 percent of the GNP applied to schooling. This compares with 5.2 percent for a random group of sixteen countries, ten of which (eight in the West) were, at one time, considered to be Christian. The range for the Muslim countries was from 5.3 percent (sub-Saharan Africa) to 1.7 percent (in South Asia). (For the United States the figure is 6.3 percent.)

Dynamics in the Contemporary Muslim World

Recent Developments in Economic Theory and Practice

As might be expected, the economic theory of Islam rests on the foundations of the Qur'an and the Sunnah. The manner in which that theory is elaborated and applied to economic development, especially in the Third World, seems to be attracting considerable attention, particularly in Muslim circles.

One systematic effort to describe the economic theory of Islam is a recent essay by Dr. Khurshid Ahmad entitled "Islam and the Challenge of Economic Development." *

The philosophical foundations of the Islamic concept of development are *tawhid* (God's unity and sovereignty), which lays down the rules for the relationship between God and human beings and between human beings; *rububiyya,* divine arrangements for nourishing, sustaining, and directing things toward their perfection; *khalifah,* the human being's role as God's viceregent on earth; and *tazkiyah,* the purification and growth of humans in all their relationships with God, with one another, with their natural environment, and with society and the state.

Dr. Ahmad's summary (p. 222) is a good definition of economic development:

> We may, therefore, submit that in an Islamic framework economic development is a goal-oriented and value-realizing activity, involving a confident and all-pervading participation of man and directed towards the maximization of human well-being in all its aspects and building the strength of the *ummah* so as to discharge in the world its role as God's viceregent on earth. . . . Development would mean moral, spiritual and material development of the individual and society leading to maximum socio-economic welfare and the ultimate good of mankind.

In economic practice, both the statist approach and the private property approach to Islamic economics are being applied in various ways in Middle Eastern countries especially. Two of these ways of application are characteristic of Islamic economics. The first concerns fiscal or monetary policies where state revenues are being channeled both to the private sector through subsidies, social services, etc., and also to development aid, through various channels, to poorer Arab countries, non-Arab countries, non-Muslim countries, and international agencies. The second concerns banking. Strictly "Islamic banks," which began to develop after 1970, operate on the

---

*In J. J. Donohue and J. L. Esposito, *Islam in Transition: Muslim Perspectives* (New York: Oxford University Press, 1982), pp. 217–222.

Islamic principle of no interest being either charged or paid on loans. By 1985 there were ten national banks and two international associations of Islamic banks with assets totaling billions of dollars, and growing rapidly. They provide all banking services for a fee that is not regarded as interest.

A Political Profile

We may approach the highly complex and dynamic political developments in the contemporary Muslim world by trying to answer four questions.

First, what is the relation between religion and political power in Islam?

Traditionally Muslims distinguish between two realms in the world: *dar al-Islam,* meaning the house of Islam and referring to "the geographical realm and true domain of Muslim faith and practice, . . . in which Islam is in full devotional, political and legal actuality," and *dar al-harb,* referring to areas of humankind as yet unsubdued by Islam, which is the house of war or "struggle unto Islamization."*

Under the secular pressures and pluralism of the modern world, however, a third realm or abode has been identified, *"dar al-sulh,* the abode of peace, where Muslims live as a minority but where they are at peace and can practice their religion freely."†

In Medina, Muhammad was at the same time Prophet and priest (leading the prayers), and ruler and commander-in-chief of the armed forces. He prepared no successor. The caliph chosen by his companions could not fill his role as "Messenger of God" but only that of "Commander of the Faithful," that is, judge, ruler, and commander-in-chief of the Muslim armies. Thus, while the religion and community of Islam gave birth to and laid the foundation of the Islamic state, the essential characteristics and constitutional structure of that state were not

---

*Kenneth Cragg, *The House of Islam,* 2nd ed. (Belmont, Calif.: Wadsworth Publishing Company, 1980), p. 128.

†S. H. Nasr, "Islam in the Islamic World Today: An Overview," in C. K. Pullapilly, ed., *Islam in the Contemporary World* (Notre Dame, Ind.: Cross Roads Books, 1980), p. 2.

laid out in the Qur'an or the Sunnah but, rather, took their form from the experience of the first four caliphates. By the end of that Golden Period of Islam the developing Islamic state had acquired the four features or characteristics that distinguished it from other state systems. They are: the concept of the rule *(hukum)* and sovereignty *(mulk)* of God, the institution of the caliphate *(khalifah)* or viceregency, the institution of consultation *(al-shura)*, and the rule of Islamic law (Shari-'ah).

These four basic characteristics provide the qualities and essential values of an Islamic state, but not its form or pattern. The Shari'ah allows for the evolution of institutions and for the realization of Islamic principles within the context of the social and temporal conditions of each Muslim country. For example, a modern representative assembly elected by universal suffrage could be one such state form, provided that the basis of the state corresponds to the fundamental principles and ideals of Islam. These principles govern Islamic polity in the interest of integrating Islamic ideology into political organizations.

Second, is there an Islamic pattern of governance in a Muslim society?

The answer, in theory, is yes; in practice, hardly. Despite the fact that a fusion of religion and political power was and remains an ideal in Muslim tradition, the absence of that fusion is a historically experienced and recognized reality. Historically, the Islamic community has lived more often than not in separate polities ruled by a wide variety of temporal authorities ranging from tribal chieftains through military regimes to modern republics.*

In discussing the role of Islam in contemporary politics, Eqbal Ahmad sees four points that deserve emphasis (p. 20):

> First, the contemporary crisis of Muslim societies is without parallel in Islamic history. Second, throughout the nineteenth and twentieth centuries the role of Islam in politics has varied in time and place. Third, the evidence of continuity with the

---

*Eqbal Ahmad, "Islam and Politics," in Yvonne Yazbeck Haddad, Byron Haines, and Ellison Findly, eds., *The Islamic Impact* (Syracuse, N.Y.: Syracuse University Press, 1984), p. 18. Used by permission.

patterns of the past has been striking. Fourth, in the 1980s the trend is toward the growth of fundamentalist, neo-totalitarian Muslim movements.

The same writer perceives three responses to the fundamental crisis in Muslim societies: restorationist, reconstructionist, and pragmatist (p. 22). They can be summarized this way:

The restorationist strives for the recovery of Islam's idealized form; an example of this is the Muslim Brotherhood in the Arab world.

The reconstructionist seeks to blend tradition with modernity in an effort to reform society. This is the thrust of the modernists, who have dominated the Muslim world both intellectually and ideologically since the middle of the nineteenth century. They include Afghani, Muhammad Abduh, Muhammad Iqbal, Mehdi Bazargan, and Abul Hasan Bani Sadr.

The pragmatist views religious requirements as being largely unrelated to the direct concerns of states and governments, and deals with the affairs of state in terms of the political and economic imperatives of contemporary life.

Third, what are the types of governance actually functioning in the thirty-eight countries where Muslims are in the majority?

As yet, no one seems to have presented a clear, detailed typology of the polities found in Muslim countries. Esposito has suggested that the pattern of a postindependence political movement in Muslim countries reveals three general orientations in government: secular, Islamic, and Muslim. At one end of the spectrum are secular states—for example, Turkey— where there is complete institutional separation of religion from politics. At the other end of the religiopolitical spectrum are the self-styled Islamic states, such as Saudi Arabia, Libya, and Pakistan, whose rulers have affirmed the Islamic character of their state and the primacy of Islamic law. The vast majority of Muslim countries, however, emerged as Muslim states, which, while remaining Western in their political, legal, and social development—as a consequence of their colonial experience—have incorporated certain Islamic trappings or constitutional provisions. In some, Islam is declared the state religion and the Shari'ah is stated to be "a" source of law, whether or not this is true in reality. Most require the head of state to be a Muslim and provide some state support or control over religious affairs. Tunisia, Algeria, Egypt, Syria, Jordan, and Malaysia reflect this approach.*

Most Muslim countries would fall in the third category. They all exemplify a struggle to establish a modern national identity and ideology within a Muslim context. Nevertheless, each country is influenced by internal and external factors rooted in the social, cultural, economic, religious, and historical realities that characterize its people.

By way of conclusion, T. W. Lippman notes, "Yet it can never be assumed that Moslems collectively will take a particular position on any issue. . . . The vision of a global Islamic community, unified in a faith that overrides ethnic, economic and linguistic differences, is as illusory now as it has been since Uthman was Caliph." He goes on to quote a prominent Muslim writer, Fazlur Rahman: "In fact, despite collective reverence for the *sunna,* and for *shari'a,* there is no generally accepted 'vision of an Islamic sociopolitical order.' "†

Fourth and last, what are the political dynamics at work in the Islamic world today?

By political dynamics is meant the forces and movements that fashion the solutions and determine the directions manifest in the Muslim world in regard to politics and government. At least five such forces can be identified.

The first is nationalism, the response to the experience of Western colonialism which created a consciousness that mobilized the people against foreign rule and eventually brought it to an end. The resulting sense of identity and of unity as a nation is part of the continuing political dynamic in the Muslim world today.

The second is socialism, which characterizes to varying de-

---

*John L. Esposito, "Muslim Societies Today," in M. Kelly, ed., *Islam: The Religious and Political Life of a World Community* (New York: Praeger, 1984), pp. 197–225.

†T. W. Lippman, *Understanding Islam: An Introduction to the Muslim World* (New York: New American Library, Mentor Books, 1982), p. 181. Used by permission.

grees the political culture of some Muslim countries, such as Egypt, Syria, and Iraq. Socialism is partly a consequence of the intervention of the West in the affairs of Islamic peoples in recent centuries. It is in some measures an expression of their rejection of or opposition to the Western capitalism that exploited them during the colonial period, and that, they feel, continues to do so in new forms. Socialism is not as significant a component in the political dynamism of the Muslim world as is nationalism, but it shows every sign of being a continuing reality in the immediate future.

Likewise, the growing strength of the third force, the Shi'ite movement, and its increasing challenge to other parts of the Islamic *ummah,* particularly the Sunni communities in Lebanon and the Gulf region, suggest that Shi'ism will continue as a militant component in the political dynamics of Islam.

Related to Shi'ism but by no means identical with it is a fourth force, the fundamentalist, neototalitarian Muslim movements that have concerns for the oppressed. Eqbal Ahmad (pp. 17–18) notes that "it is difficult to recall a widely-known Muslim saint who did not collide with state power," and "In its exemplary form, Islam is a religion of the oppressed."

Those dynamics manifested so prominently today are well conveyed by the following excerpt from Eqbal Ahmad (p. 25):

> For the majority of Muslim peoples, the experienced alternative to the past is limbo—of foreign occupation, and dispossession, of alienation from the land, of life in shanty-towns and refugee camps, of migration into foreign lands, and, at best, of permanent expectancy. . . . Hence, in our time, religiously oriented millenarian movements have tended to be harbingers of revolution. . . . The often publicized ideological resurgence of Islam . . . is a product of excessive, uneven modernization and the failure of governments to safeguard national sovereignty or to satisfy basic needs. In "transitional" third world societies, one judges the present *morally,* with reference to the past, to inherited values, but *materially* in relation to the future. Therein lies a new dualism in our social and political life; the inability or unwillingness to deal with it entails disillusionment, terrible costs, and possible tragedy. One mourns Iran, laments Pakistan, fears for Egypt.

Islamic Revivalism

Let us now examine what seems to be happening in the contemporary world of Islam, principally the phenomenon that is variously referred to as "Resurgent Islam," "Islamic Revivalism," "Islamization," and "Re-Islamization" by the growing number of writers on the subject. The variety yet relatedness of these terms suggests that the phenomenon is quite complex. As the following definition makes clear, Islamic revivalism involves not just religion and politics but also economic, social, and cultural dimensions, some aspects of which have generated considerable emotional and spiritual energy.

First, a definition of the phenomenon by a sympathetic Western (Christian) scholar is helpful:

> Islamic revivalism in its broadest sense refers to the renewal of Islam in Muslim personal and public life. Its manifestations include an increase in religious observances . . . ; a revitalization of sufi . . . orders; proliferation of religious publications and media programming; calls for the implementation of Islamic law; the creation of Islamic banks; and the growth of Islamic organizations and activist movements.
>
> . . . Islamic revivalism has led to the reassertion of Islam in politics. . . .
>
> The forms that Islamic revivalism takes vary almost infinitely from one country to another, but there are certain recurrent themes: a sense that existing political, economic and social systems have failed, a disenchantment with and even a rejection of the West; a quest for identity and greater authenticity; and the conviction that Islam provides a self-sufficient ideology for state and society, a valid alternative to secular nationalism, socialism and capitalism.*

A second Western analysis of Islamic revivalism is found in an article on "The Anatomy of Islamic Revival" by R. H. Dekmejian,† who attempts to identify some of the characteristics of the movement and to discern the possible causal factors.

---

*John L. Esposito, *Islamic Revivalism: The Muslim World Today,* Occasional Paper No. 5 (Washington, D.C.: American Institute for Islamic Affairs, American University, 1985), p. 1.

†*The Middle East Journal,* vol. 34, no. 1 (Winter 1980), pp. 1–12.

First, he notes three basic attributes of Islamic revival: its pervasiveness, being a transnational phenomenon; its polycentrism, having no single epicenter; and its persistence, having existed over the last century in a dialectical movement between Islam and secularism.

He then suggests that Islamic revival is a response to felt crisis in three broad categories:

• A perceived legitimacy crisis together with insufficiently effectual leadership
• A perceived paucity of social justice in Muslim countries
• The persistence of military defeats

Three areas of social activity that correspond to the three catalytic factors of the contemporary crisis are then suggested:

• A return to the traditional Islamic formula of legitimization and true Islamic leadership
• The notion that social justice is strongly embedded in Islamic conscience and consciousness
• Islam's positive attitude toward military success and prowess, emphasizing such concepts as *jihad* (struggle on behalf of God), *qhazi* (victory), *shahid* (martyrdom in the name of Islam), and *izzah* (honor).

Dr. Khurshid Ahmad, a Pakistani Muslim, provides a third analysis of Islamic revivalism. He approaches the phenomenon from within the Islamic context and against the background of colonial experience, the more than 200-year British rule of the Indian subcontinent. He sees four results of that experience:

• The secularization of Muslim social, political, and economic institutions
• The development of a pattern of dependence on the West
• The bifurcation of education into two streams: modern secular education, creating modern secular elites, and traditional religious education, producing traditional religious elites

• A crisis of leadership—foreign political leaders having displaced traditional Muslim leaders, with the result that foreign-oriented local leadership was not trusted by the Muslim community

Two basic strategies for revival emerged in answer to the question, Why did this happen?

The first strategy was that of the modernists, who said that times had changed and Muslims must take the values, technology, and institutions of the ruling power.

A second strategy was that of the revival movements, who said that revival was necessary because Muslims were not true to Islam; they had left their base. This produced two responses: (1) that of the traditionalists, who advocate a return to true Islam in order to preserve the Islamic legacy, and (2) that of the reconstructionists, who strive to rebuild society and its institutions in light of the Islamic milieu.

It is essential to look at the Islamic revivalist movements and seek to understand them in light of their own perceptions of their role. Certain common characteristics emerge.

> The most important aspect of the mission of these Islamic movements has been their emphasis on Islam, not just a set of beliefs and rituals, but as a moral and social movement to establish an Islamic order. . . . These Islamic movements seek for comprehensive reform, that is, changing all aspects of life, making faith the centre point.*

Also notable is that the thrust of Islamic revival is not nationalistic in character. Islam is ideological in nature and is by definition international, a universal religion.

Revivalism is also nonsectarian; it tries to bring all sects and schools of Muslim thought to common ground.

Finally (p. 224), it seeks to act as a bridge between the modern and the conservative, between the old and the new, between the Westernizing and the traditional.

---

*Khurshid Ahmad, "The Nature of Islamic Resurgence," in J. L. Esposito, ed., *Voices of Resurgent Islam* (New York: Oxford University Press, 1983), pp. 222, 223.

The movement clearly differentiates between development and modernization, on the one hand, and secularization and Westernization on the other. It says "yes" to modernization but "no" to blind Westernization. . . . It is the profound feeling of the Muslim people that the Western experiment has failed. Both its variants, the capitalistic as well as the socialistic, have been tried and found wanting.

This overall profile of the Muslim world concludes with a statement (pp. 228–229) that is particularly apropos to most readers of this book.

I would like to invite my Western colleagues to understand that Muslim criticism of Western civilization is not an exercise in political confrontation. The real competition would be at the level of the two cultures and civilizations, one based on Islamic values and the other on the values of materialism and nationalism. Had Western culture been based on Christianity, on morality and faith, the language and *modus operandi* of the contact would have been different. But that is not the case. The choice is between the Divine Principle and secular, materialistic culture. And there is no reason to believe that this competition should be seen in terms of the geo-politic boundaries of the West and the East. In fact, all those human beings who are concerned over the spiritual and moral crisis of our times should heave a sigh of relief over Islamic resurgence, and not be scared or put off by it. . . . There is nothing pathologically anti-Western in the Muslim resurgence. . . . If China and the United States and Russia and India can have friendly relations without sharing common culture and politico-economic system, why not the West and the Muslim world? *Much depends on how the West looks upon this phenomenon of Islamic resurgence and wants to come to terms with it.* If in the Muslim mind and the Muslim viewpoint, Western powers remain associated with efforts to perpetuate the Western model in Muslim society, keeping Muslims tied to the system of Western domination at national and international levels and thus destabilizing Muslim culture and society directly or indirectly, then, of course, tension will increase. Differences are bound to multiply. And if things are not resolved peacefully through dialogue and understanding, through respect for each other's rights and genuine concerns, they are destined to be resolved otherwise. But if, on the other hand, we can acknowledge and accept that this world is a pluralistic world, that Western culture can co-exist with other cultures and civilizations without expecting to dominate over them, that others need not necessarily be looked upon as enemies or foes, but as potential friends, then there is a genuine possibility that we can learn to live with our differences. If we are prepared to follow this approach, then we would be able to discover many a common ground and many a common challenge. Otherwise I am afraid we are heading for hard times.

4

Studies of Four Countries

NIGERIA

Nigeria is located on the west coast of Africa just above the equator. Comprising 356,669 square miles, it is somewhat larger than Texas and Oklahoma together. Today it is the most populous and affluent nation of sub-Saharan Africa with the exception of South Africa. Though population estimates vary, 90 to 100 million people live in Nigeria, with an annual growth rate of nearly 2.5 percent. This makes Nigeria overwhelmingly a nation of young people, with about 45 percent of the population fifteen years or younger. Of the population, around 45 percent are Muslim, 45 percent are Christian, and 9 percent belong to African traditional religions. Again, estimates of this division vary, often along ideological lines.

The geography of Nigeria varies from the semiarid sub-Saharan grasslands of the north to the great rain forests, swamps, and river basins along the Atlantic Ocean in the South. The northern region, while the largest geographically, is the most sparsely populated. The converse is true of the south. Because of its fertility and development, the economic wealth of Nigeria is in the south. The affluence of the country is due mainly to the development of the oil industry in the south in the late 1960s.

The full report for the Nigeria case study was the result of the research and writing of Donald G. Dawe, a member of the Islamic Study Advisory Committee.

Precolonial Nigeria was an area of great and dynamic movements of peoples. As a result, it has today over 500 languages. The modern state of Nigeria did not take shape until it was consolidated by the British in 1914. Under British rule the country was divided into three regions shaped by natural boundaries and tribal dominions. The Hausa and Fulani peoples control the northern region, which is solidly Muslim. The southern region was divided into a western section, partly Christian and partly Muslim, dominated by the Yoruba tribe, and an eastern section, mainly Christian, dominated by the Ibo. Colonial control was strongest in the south along the coastline. The northern region experienced considerable political independence.

After national independence in 1960, political control changed hands several times, from the establishment of the First Republic at the time of independence to the present rule of Major General Ibrahim Babangida and a twenty-eight-member Supreme Military Council. All leaders have had to deal with an unstable economy, corruption in high places, power struggles of various kinds, and regional, tribal, and religious sectarianism. When the price of oil was high, the affluence of the country eased these tensions somewhat. However, the current decline in oil income has exacerbated these problems.

The Nigerians are religious people, having a strong sense of identity with their particular religious traditions and communities. The two largest communities are the Muslim and the Christian. Religious identity for Nigerians is very much intertwined with geographical, tribal, regional, economic, and political factors.

The Muslim Community and Islam

Of the two major religions, Islam was the first to come to Nigeria. As early as the ninth century, Berber Muslim merchants led trade expeditions to cities in the northern region. These and later trade involvements led to the conversion of merchants and the ruling classes. Kano became the influential Muslim city of the north. From these beginnings, Islam spread gradually southward and westward into the Yorubaland.

A major event in the growth of Islam was the establishment of the Sokoto caliphate in the early 1800s by a Fulani leader, Shehu Uthman, and Fodio, who initiated a *jihad*. In this caliphate Sunni Islam, with its law of the Shari'ah, was the normative law of the land and brought religious purity in the north. It was headed by a Hausa-Fulani elite that shaped and continues to shape the area to the present day. Because they live in a more pluralistic society, Muslims in the south have not lived under governments whose fundamental law is the Shari'ah. Nor do they dominate social, political, and economic life. This provides for a measure of accommodation and integration in the south that is not found in the north. However, forces at work today within the Muslim community are increasingly calling such accommodation into question.

During the colonial period Islam continued to grow. It reached its maximum growth in the 1950s and 1960s, when it presented itself as an African religion for Africans against Christianity, which was the white man's religion of colonialism. Since independence, the growth rate of Islam has equaled that of the population as a whole. Within its long history, movements of renewal and reform have reshaped Nigerian Islam. As in other parts of the Muslim world, Sufi fellowships were established. During the 1960s and 1970s, these fellowships facilitated the integration of the Islam of northern Nigeria into the mainstream of modern Nigerian life and the spread of Islam throughout the whole of Nigeria. There also exist a number of more heterodox groups that seek to integrate Islam more closely into a culture now shaped by Western education and modern technology. Lately these movements of accommodation have come under attack.

In the mid-1970s the Izala movement, a society for the "rooting out of innovation (heresy)," was established. This reform movement struggles to purify Islam and Muslim society of all modernization that is contrary to what it considers to be orthodox Islam. Its members are strongly critical of the moral decadence, use of drugs and alcohol, and sexual promiscuity associated with the affluence and secular life found in many Nigerian cities and with the influence of Western culture upon Nigeria. Their stance brings them into conflict with any Islamic accommodation to culture and social change that is contrary to their orthodoxy, and with Christianity, which from their point of view is a traditional carrier of Western colonialism and culture into Nigeria. This movement appeals strongly to many Nigerians, especially the young, who are concerned to make Nigeria an Islamic nation.

Nigerian Islam is also influenced today by the movement of those who expect a coming Mahdi, or teacher of righteousness. The Mahdi will inaugurate the true Islamic society and thus bring an end to social injustices and economic difficulties. In the past, Nigerians have identified several leaders as the Mahdi. One such person was the charismatic Muhammadu Marwa, popularly called "Maitatsine," who proclaimed a reformed Islam that was to prepare people morally and spiritually for the final day of judgment. He formed communes of revolutionary reform that engaged in acts of civil disobedience and crime, which led finally to his death at the hands of the Nigerian army in 1980. The Maitatsine movement affected some Muslims deeply, although it was opposed by the leadership of both the Sufi fellowships and the Izala movement. The dislocated urban poor, fresh from the country in search of livelihood, found the Maitatsine solution appealing. The possibility for a reemergence of this movement remains.

While often divided by movements antagonistic toward each other, the Muslim community of Nigeria is able to accept considerable divergence within and yet demonstrate to the outsider a unity of faith and purpose that Christians do not enjoy. Because the government supported the participation of Nigerians in the Hajj, the annual pilgrimage, thousands have gone to Mecca. This participation has reinforced their sense of solidarity with the whole Muslim world and brought them into contact with centers of orthodoxy in the Middle East. This has increased within the Nigerian Muslim community a deep desire to have a nation that is governed by Islamic principles and characterized by Islamic social order and custom.

Christianity

Christianity was introduced to Nigeria during the colonial period by European and American missionaries, both Protestant and Roman Catholic. As was the case with Islam, converts to this new religion came mostly from those people who formerly had been adherents of an African traditional religion. Since colonial rule was most strongly felt in the south along the coast, this was the area in which Christianity grew in relative isolation from the Muslim north. As with Islam, it was able to identify with the tribal structures and ethnic groups of the nation, though the churches were patterned after the Western churches of the missionaries. Missionaries established educational institutions and hospitals and conducted social and evangelistic work. Mission schools trained a corps of people to conduct the business and political affairs of the country, giving Christians a decided advantage over Muslims with respect to employment in these two areas. With independence, the growth of the Christian community entered a new phase. Nigerian Christians are now in charge of the affairs of their churches. Most of the Protestant churches of "missionary" origin now work together within the context of the Christian Council of Churches or the Christian Association of Nigeria.

During the colonial period the growth of the Christian community was slow but steady. Since 1960, several developments have had an extraordinary effect on the growth of the church. One of these is the establishment of a number of indigenous independent churches. These independent churches are completely of national origin and not dependent upon Western missionaries and denominations. They have a charismatic leadership and worship, with an emphasis upon healing and the gifts of the Holy Spirit, and demonstrate an openness to indigenous forms of worship and life. Since political independence these churches have experienced rapid growth. Today somewhere between 10 and 15 percent of Nigerians are related to one of these independent churches.

Within the more mission-related churches, the Church Growth movement, with its emphasis upon the conversion of "homogeneous" human groups rather than isolated individuals, claims some success in bringing heretofore unresponsive tribal groups, most notably the Tiv tribe, into the Christian fold.

As in the United States, the charismatic renewal of the church has had a strong impact upon Nigerian churches and has brought fresh vitality to church life and accelerated the process of indigenization.

Like the Muslim community, the Christian community is also concerned about the social, political, and economic problems confronting the country, the breakdown of moral standards, and continuing corruption in high places. For the church, however, the impact of Western culture and technology upon the life of the nation does not present the same kinds of problems as it does for the Muslim community. The churches of Nigeria are committed to life in a religiously plural society with a separation of church and state. The source of social justice is not found in a religious system or Christian theocracy but in a change of the human heart and mind.

Relationships Between Christians and Muslims

Since independence Nigerians have been struggling to develop a nation that is politically sound and economically viable. Further, they want it to be the embodiment of what they are as a people, both culturally and religiously. Because Nigeria is a highly diverse nation, its pursuit of these national goals has moved along a rocky road. Different tribal loyalties, religious identities, political theories, and social orientations have produced sharp controversy, and these continue to foster struggles for political and economic power and even civil war. The causes of these factors are complex and difficult to understand. All affect the relationships between the Christian and Muslim communities.

Though Christians and Muslims have worked to establish a modern, technologically oriented nation-state, a number of events have occurred that have undermined cooperation and goodwill and have influenced the perception Christians and Muslims have of one another. The first of these was the Civil War in 1967. This war was precipitated by the secession of the

southeastern part of Nigeria to form Biafra. This area is dominated by the Ibo tribe with its Christian majority and is the area
in which the oil is located. An important factor leading to this
war was the 1966–67 pogrom in northern Nigeria against the
Ibo businessmen and government officials who, with the advantage of Western education in mission schools, had taken
jobs in the north. The war did not solve the problem, though
efforts have been made by the government to reintegrate the
nation. Also, as a result of the war, some Christian missionaries
who had stayed with their schools and congregations in Biafra
were expelled from the country. Since then the Nigerian government has made it more difficult for missionaries to obtain
visas and residence permits. A number of leaders in the church
view this as evidence of Muslim influence upon government
policy.

A more critical matter is that of the different understandings
of statehood. Many Christians are convinced that the Muslim
community wants the nation to be governed by the Islamic
Shari'ah, as was the practice in northern Nigeria in the days of
British control. Under the Shari'ah, every non-Muslim is relegated to a "protected people" *(dhimmi)* status, which they
perceive as making them second-class citizens. Some Muslim
groups do advocate this position. No government, however,
even those with Muslim leadership, has yet accepted that specific proposal. Muslims did propose the creation of a Federal
Shari'ah Court, but the proposal was defeated. Some Christians
continue to fear that the ultimate goal of the Muslim community is an Islamic state of Nigeria wherein Christians would not
enjoy full citizenship.

Other proposals and actions of the government also nourish
these fears. The support given by the government to Muslim
participation in the Hajj, the (unsuccessful) proposal by one
government to establish an Islamic Affairs Board, and the na-
tionalization of a number of Christian hospitals and mission
schools causes anxiety among Christians. In addition, the burn-
ing of churches in Kano following the visits of the Pope and
of Anglican Archbishop Robert Runcie to northern Nigeria,
as well as problems encountered in obtaining missionary visas,
importing Bibles, and teaching Christian religious knowledge;

issues pertaining to the property rights of churches; and the ban on public preaching, all lead Christians to ponder what their future in Nigeria is going to be.

On the other side, many Muslims question what their future would be in the kind of open democratic state that Christians seem to endorse. In such a state, they perceive the loss of their identity as Muslims, an erosion of their cultural tradition, and an enhancement of the moral degeneration now prevalent under secular governments. These perceptions are related by many Muslims to the desire to gain the power and control in government and business that Christians exercised in the colonial period and in the early days of independence. Muslims seek a more equitable balance of power to redress the discrimination they have endured in the past. Further, they do not view the role of the Western Christian missionary in this struggle as passive and neutral. On the contrary, they view the evangelistic strategies of many Western missionaries as provocative and deliberate, having the implicit intent to undermine Islam and to foster the hegemony of Western culture and religion over Nigerian life.

The relationships between the Muslim and Christian communities involve very serious issues. They have to do with the nature of the state, religious authority and freedom, political structures, and economic power. Both communities struggle with regional and tribal loyalties in a nation-state, and the adjustment of traditional African life to Western culture and technology. Many Christians and Muslims are working together to resolve these issues in spite of the tensions that prevail. This effort should not be underestimated. Both Christians and Muslims feel, however, that their relationship has been undermined by foreign intervention. Christians attribute the increasing Muslim emphasis upon Islamic orthodoxy to the increasing presence of the Arab petrodollar. Muslims see the Christian community as being used as a means of exploitation by the Western, capitalistic, secular, materialistic forces of colonialism.

Christian evangelism and Muslim *da'wah,* no matter how well intended, also create problems for relationships. Over the past years, people belonging to African traditional religions have converted to the Christian faith and to Islam. The conversion of Christians to Islam and Muslims to Christianity has been negligible, despite claims to the contrary. The problem is that each community sees the other as using unethical and coercive measures to gain converts. For example, both Christians and Muslims use some apologetic literature that contains distorting polemics and outmoded arguments. Some Christian mission groups still talk of "crusades" to take over whole areas for Christ. Muslims understand this not as a spiritual movement but as a political threat. Ironically, some Christians find it equally threatening when some Muslims use the same "missionary" strategies in their work to convert Christians. An interesting exception to this conflict is a very small group of Muslims who call themselves "Isawa," which means "disciples of Jesus." They are faithful Muslims who take seriously the Qur'anic belief in Jesus as a prophet. However, their impact upon the relationships between Christians and Muslims is negligible.

The future of Christian–Muslim relations in Nigeria will depend to a considerable degree upon the ability of both communities to address these problems together and to find equitable solutions. In both communities there are those working toward this objective who recognize that accommodation from both sides will be necessary. Belief in the Lordship of God allows them to hope that each will find within its own understanding of faithfulness to God that resolution which will bring peace and justice to their nation.

INDONESIA

Indonesia, the fifth most populous nation in the world, claims more Muslims than any other country. The 1987 population is estimated to become 167.5 million, and approximately 87.5 percent, or 146.5 million, will be Muslim. This is slightly less than all the Muslims in the Middle East. Eight to

This section is a condensation of a paper prepared by Frank L. Cooley, staff of the Islamic Study Advisory Committee.

nine percent, or 13.9 million, are Christian; the remainder embrace Hinduism, Buddhism, or indigenous religion. Indonesia is a nation of islands that extend over 3,000 miles from east to west and over 1,100 miles from north to south. Of all the countries in the region of Southern Asia, it was also under European domination the longest. A brief summary of its history will set the stage for understanding the relationships between Muslims and Christians in the life of Indonesia.

For our purposes, the historical background of Indonesia begins with the coming of Indian traders in the twelfth century. They established permanent Muslim settlements on the westernmost islands, which were ruled by Hindu princes. The strong presence of Buddhism and, especially, Hinduism in western Indonesia for at least a millennium prior to Islam's taking root among the people, has indelibly marked the character of the Muslim community that has developed there.

One of the earliest Islamic settlements began in 1204, in Aceh in North Sumatra. From there Islam spread to Java, over which Muslim sultans ruled by the end of the sixteenth century.

The importance of these islands for trade and commerce did not pass unnoticed by European nations. By 1292 Marco Polo had already visited Indonesia. The Portuguese conquered Malacca in 1511. This marked the beginning of colonial presence in the islands and the introduction of Roman Catholicism to the area. Portuguese control continued until the coming of the Dutch East India Company in 1605. In the early nineteenth century the Dutch colonial government replaced the bankrupt company. By 1910 this government had control of all of the East Indies. The Westernization of the islands had begun. Dutch rule finally ended with a defeat by the Indonesians during the struggle for independence (1945–1949) which followed the harsh Japanese occupation of 1942 to 1945.

With Independence, the modern period of Indonesian history begins. From 1950 to 1959 a European-style parliamentary democracy under the leadership of President Sukarno was tried. Because this government did not provide security, stability, and national unity, it was dissolved in 1959 by Sukarno, who established a "guided democracy" and "guided econ-

omy" operating under a constitution drafted in 1945. The next
six years likewise failed to bring national unity, political stability, or economic growth. An attempted coup in 1965 was
quickly put down by the armed forces and attributed by them
to the Communist Party. This led to widespread killings and
disappearances of those charged with being affiliated or in
sympathy with the Communists. As a result of all this, Sukarno
lost power, and in March 1966 the reins of government were
transferred to General Suharto, who had led the army in putting down the coup. The army became the real center of
power. The ensuing period was labeled by its leaders the
"New Order," the "Old Order" being the period of Sukarno's
rule, 1950–1965.

A determinative event in the history of relations between
Christians and Muslims was the adoption of the Pancasila (Five
Pillars). They are: belief in unitary deity, nationalism,
humanitarianism, representative democracy, and social justice
for all Indonesians. The formulation of the first pillar avoided
giving preference to any one particular religion. As a result,
Islam, Christianity, Hinduism, and Buddhism are all recognized as official religions of Indonesia. Enacted by consensus
in August 1945 as the foundation of the Indonesian state, the
Pancasila has continued in force until the present. In 1985, the
New Order Government expanded the scope and authority of
the Pancasila to make it the sole basis of social and political
activity of all mass organizations, including those under the
banner of religion. However, this expanded authority does not
apply to narrowly defined religious organizations like
churches, mosques, and temple congregations.

The Muslim Community

After taking root in Indonesia in the twelfth century, the
Muslim community grew gradually and steadily, following the
expansion of trade and political power throughout the islands.
Once established, Islamization generally proceeded peaceably
though accompanied by a constant struggle between the principles of Islam and the deep-rooted Javanism, which was a synthesis of Hinduism and Buddhism with indigenous religion.

The coming of the Portuguese and the Dutch did not halt the expansion of Islam. If anything, Western rule and Dutch colonial policies that kept religious communities relatively separate may have aided in its expansion.

In the early 1900s, Muslims began to form Islamic organizations of various kinds. Some like Serikat Islam (1905), later the Partai Serikat Islam Indonesia, the United Indonesian Islamic Party (PSII, established in 1930), were committed to Indonesian nationalism. Others pursued different objectives. The Muhammadiyah, founded in 1912 as a nonpolitical social organization, stressed the adaptation of Islamic principles in order to meet the challenge of Western secular thinking. It represented those people now identified as "modernists." In the early 1920s the Persatuan Islam (Persis) was organized to teach and spread Islam. The Nahdlatul Ulama (Revival of the Scribes) was established in 1926 as the political forum of the traditionalists and advocates of traditional Islamic values in the developing national life of Indonesia as it became modernized.

In the mix of the organizations just identified, there are represented the divisions within the Muslim community over the way in which Islam is to be practiced. The modernists and the traditionalists are two of the contenders. A third consisted of those Muslims who were secular, Western-educated, and politically oriented civil servants and intelligentsia. From this group came many leaders of the nationalist movement. This is the grouping that has joined with the army to "guide" the development of Indonesia today.

The traditionalists and the modernists were concerned with the Islamic character of Indonesia and with Muslim participation in the affairs of state. These groups and their concerns are the key to understanding Muslim political activity in Indonesia today. Even before World War II Muslim organizations began to formulate political thought to advance their concerns. The Japanese invasion ended these efforts. But with independence in 1945, the Pancasila was adopted, frustrating once again the desire of some Muslims for an Islamic state. When the 1965 coup was attempted, Muslims cooperated with the military to eliminate the Communists and their sympathizers, expecting to gain for themselves the political power that the Communists had enjoyed under Sukarno's rule. The army, however, rebuffed them in the interest of defending the Pancasila. As a result, many Muslims feel that they, as the majority community, have been deprived of a political role that is rightfully theirs.

Several other considerations also aid in understanding the Muslim community. Since Independence, the Muslims' sense of belonging to the world community of Islam has grown markedly. This has resulted from their increasing participation in the Hajj, their importing and translating the writings of Muslim modernists and revivalists of Pakistan and the Middle East, the influx of foreign money to help build mosques and Islamic institutions and to support various outreach programs, and contacts with Muslims of other countries made by those studying and traveling abroad.

Apart from the political positions just outlined, the Javanese Muslim community exhibits other differences. There are the more orthodox Muslims called Santri, the more heterodox, syncretistic Muslims called Abangan, and the aristocratic intelligentsia called Priyayi. The traditionalists are more likely to be represented by the Santri group (though many younger Santris are modernists), while secular nationalists are found mostly in the Abangan and Priyayi groups. In general, Santri Muslims have supported the ideal of an Islamic state; while Abangan and Priyayi Muslims actively support Pancasila government and Javanese culture and customs in general. All of them tend to observe Javanese *adat* (the indigenous system of social control).

There is an increased emphasis upon *da'wah*, stimulated by the impact of the materialistic, secular values of the West upon the country, which many Indonesians feel has been encouraged by the development policies of the government, by widely publicized reports about the "flood of conversions" to Christianity in Indonesia following the coup of 1965, and by the unwillingness of the government to halt Christian attempts at conversion.

Finally, because of the inability of organized Islamic political movements to gain a major role in government, there is evidence that more radical forms of Islamic political activity are appearing. The government is alert to these developments and has taken strong measures both to forestall them and to prosecute those engaging in them.

The Christian Community

Perhaps the greatest problem facing the Christian community in Indonesia is the impression that others have of it as a foreign element in Indonesian society. Unlike Islam, Christianity was introduced and is perceived to have grown under the umbrella of colonial power. The establishment of the Roman Catholic Church, originally primarily in the Moluccas, coincided with the arrival in that area of the Portuguese at the beginning of the sixteenth century. When the Dutch trading interests replaced the Portuguese, the door was opened for the introduction of Reformed Protestantism, whose chief enemy in Europe at the time was the Roman Catholic Church. Muslim rulers did not welcome the coming of Christianity. Not wanting religious problems to interfere with their trading interests, initially the Dutch rulers remained, for the most part, neutral with respect to religious issues. For example, Christian missionaries were allowed to come but their work was generally limited to areas where indigenous religion, rather than Islam or Hinduism, was dominant. The Muslim community benefited from this policy because it allowed Islam to expand unopposed into the interior sections of Java and Sumatra. In the latter part of the colonial period, Dutch officials became more favorably disposed toward the Christian church. The Dutch government had subsidized the salaries of pastors and teachers of the Protestant Church of the Indies from the beginning, however.

The 1980 statistical picture shows a Roman Catholic Church of 3.8 million people, or 29.5 percent of the Christian population of Indonesia; 55 conciliar Protestant churches, joined together in the Communion of Churches in Indonesia and consisting of 7.1 million people, or 55 percent; Pentecostal churches with a membership of 1 million, or 7.75 percent; and nonconciliar, non-Pentecostal churches, which consider themselves to be "evangelical" rather than "ecumenical," with nearly 1 million, or 7.75 percent. Over half of the evangelical churches were established by foreign missionaries after 1965, with some of their membership coming from the older church groups.

In the pre-independence period, a number of Christians were deeply involved in the nationalist movement. This involvement was related to the struggle of many Protestant churches to obtain autonomy from the state-supported church of the Dutch, and also independence from the domination of Western missionaries and Western church organizations. Their struggle was aided by the Japanese invasion, at which time Western presence was eliminated.

When independence came, a significant segment of the Christian community participated fully in the development of the new nation. Not only had it fought the Dutch in the struggle for independence, it gave its support to the governments that have followed. For example, Christians, as over against the Muslim community, generally advocated the Pancasila. In later years, the church, though continuing to cooperate with the government, did voice disagreement with government attempts in 1978 and 1979 to restrict the propagation of religion and to limit or control overseas assistance to religious institutions. As a result, the government has not carried through with these attempts. Then in 1985 the church, along with Muslim organizations, expressed concern about the application of the Pancasila to religious organizations.

In 1950 the churches, concerned for the unity of the church and of their country, formed the Council of Churches in Indonesia. Under the leadership of this council, the churches established ties with the World Council of Churches and have remained active participants in that body even at the risk of being accused once again of being foreign. As evidence of this growing ecumenism, the conciliar Protestant churches and the Roman Catholic Church have come closer together, working side by side on many issues.

This growing spirit of unity has been challenged since 1965 by the dramatic increase in the presence and activities of foreign (not just Western) conservative evangelists and parachurch agencies. Their work has offended older churches because they have lost members to the new missionary churches. Their missionaries have offended other religious groups by their ignorance of the situation, their aggressive, insensitive approach, and their "Christian" chauvinism.

In addition to these concerns, the churches have been critical of the materialistic and immoral aspects of the modernization process. This agrees with much of the Muslim criticism of Westernization.

Finally, Christians are concerned about any attempt on the part of Muslims to change Indonesia into an Islamic state or to make the Shari'ah law normative. Their fears in this matter have been influenced by the memory of the Dar-ul-Islam rebellion in 1950, which was motivated by the desire of some Muslims to establish an Islamic state. They also fear what they perceive to be the impact of Islamic revivalism upon some Muslim groups.

Relationships Between Christians and Muslims

Muslims and Christians in Indonesia have, for many years, been adversaries. This was caused in part by their ignorance of each other, an ignorance fostered by the separatist policies of the Dutch colonialists. The Christian churches also inherited Western attitudes toward Islam and Muslims. From the Muslim point of view, Christians were the favorites, at Muslim expense, of both the colonial and national governments, in spite of these governments' declared neutrality with respect to religions. Other factors have complicated Christian–Muslim relations. During the first fifteen years of the Old Order, fanatical guerrilla forces in West and Central Java and in South Sulawesi waged terrorist attacks with the aim of establishing an Islamic state in the new republic. Since Islamic political parties did not repudiate these efforts, though they did not support them either, the clear impression was given (to those non-Muslims susceptible to it) that their future was threatened by a militant Muslim community committed to changing the foundations of the Indonesian state.

Relationships in the period of the New Order have been affected by the response to the coup of September 30, 1965, which was attributed to the Communist Party. Shortly after the coup, the Communist Party was outlawed and all Indonesians were advised to choose a religion. Failure to do this meant that one was a Communist, in which case either death or imprisonment might follow. The result was a large-scale movement of people into Islam, Hinduism, and Christianity. Dramatic reporting by Western media of mass conversions of Indonesians to the Christian faith aroused strong negative reactions within the Muslim community. This, in turn, led to attempts by the government in the late 1960s to get the two communities to agree to cease using the other as a target in their propagation. This attempt failed on the grounds that it constrained both faiths from carrying out their religious duty.

Aware of Muslim feelings about the constraints imposed on their participation in government, the New Order has sought to demonstrate to Muslim groups the government concern for them by giving, for example, through the Department of Religion, financial support to Muslim institutions of higher education and for religious instruction. Since Christian institutions have not benefited equally, some Christians feel that this department is strongly biased toward the Muslim community.

Because both the Christian faith and Islam are concerned to propagate their beliefs, the relationship between Christian mission and Islamic *da'wah* is of importance to the two communities. The regulating factor in this relationship has been the government, which has ruled that relations between the religions must be handled in such a way as to shun open contradictions in the efforts of religious adherents to carry out their calling to mission and *da'wah*. In this connection, the expression "Religious communities must create harmonious relations in society" has become popular in recent years. As a result, the relationship between mission and *da'wah* has not been a serious issue within Indonesia.

The unique aspect of the interfaith situation is the active participation of the government in religious affairs as a "neutral" party. Its concern is for peace, harmony, and stability. The country will not advance and develop if it is disrupted by internal strife. In response to this concern many Christian and Muslim leaders have worked together to achieve this harmony.

Christians have emphasized themes of tolerance, dialogue, and cooperation in an effort to encourage the church to participate positively in the achievement of harmony. Some Muslim leaders have initiated similar efforts within their own communities. In addition, numerous interfaith consultations have been held between Christian and Muslim leaders. Further, these leaders have attended the international dialogue programs sponsored by the World Council of Churches and other agencies. It is this development which is a harbinger of what the future of relations between the two groups might be. With the right kind of government involvement and encouragement, Christians and Muslims in Indonesia might become an example for others who in their own situations are looking forward to the development of better relations between the religious communities.

EGYPT

Egypt, the land of the Nile, is a country whose history and civilization reach back into earliest recorded time. With a present population of around 49 million people, 91 percent of whom are Muslim and 9 percent Christian, it is the most populous country in the Middle East. The history of the Christian community in Egypt goes back, according to tradition, to the ministry of Mark in the first century A.D. When the religion of Islam was introduced by the invading Muslim armies in the seventh century, Christianity was the religion of Egypt. Since that time, the Christian community has gradually decreased to its present size, becoming as a result a minority community. Islam, on the other hand, has become the religion of the majority. This change is all the more difficult for Christians since Islam came to Egypt almost five hundred years after the Christian community had established itself as the majority. The history of this change reflects cycles of tolerance and tension in the relationships between the two communities. At no time

This section has been developed from two longer papers, one by Victor E. Makari of the Islamic Study Advisory Committee and the other by Wadi Z. Haddad.

have the relations been easy. In order to understand the current situation between Christians and Muslims in Egypt, we must take a brief look at history.

Historical Background

During the early centuries of the Christian era, the great majority of Egyptians embraced the Christian faith, some in opposition to the will of Greek and Roman rulers. The church they established became known as the Coptic Orthodox Church, "Coptic" being another word for "Egyptian." Though persecuted by Rome, the Christian community produced in Alexandria one of the major centers of Christian learning. The church fathers Clement (d. 220) and Origen (d. 254) came from that center. In the midst of the great Christological controversies of the third century, the Coptic Church upheld the monophysite view, a position rejected by the Council of Chalcedon. This led the Byzantine emperors, who ruled over them, to persecute the Coptic Church because of its "heresy." The response of the Christian community was martyrdom and monasticism. Because of the character of this latter movement, many Muslims accused the Christian community of being unconcerned about the affairs of this world.

In 641 deliverance came in the form of Muslim invaders from Arabia, who brought welcome relief from over two centuries of oppression by the Byzantines. The early Muslim rulers granted *dhimmi* status to the Christians. This gave the Christians security in life and property, freedom to practice their religion, and exemption from military service, in return for the payment of a special tax. The early Muslim rulers were friendly and provided a great degree of justice for Christians. Historical, political, and military changes, created by internal rivalry and conflicts among Muslims themselves, resulted in alternating regimes with varying degrees of tolerance toward Christians. During the seventh and eighth centuries many Christians converted to Islam, some to avoid a special tax, some to gain an economic or social advantage, and some because Islam held more relevance for them. In spite of the toleration shown to them by Muslim rulers, the Christians in general felt that they had an inferior status in their own country. This feeling was enhanced by the immigrations of Arab peoples, because this meant a diminishing proportion of Christians in Egypt.

The coming of the Shi'ite Fatimids in 969 saw a continuation of these relationships. The Fatimid rulers relied upon the expertise and honesty of their Christian subjects in assessing and collecting taxes, in administrating state finance, and in medical care. During these centuries Muslim leaders made no effort to convert people by coercion, the one exception being Caliph al-Hakim, whom even Muslims despised for his cruelty.

The Fatimid rule was ended in 1171 by the Sunni leader Saladin, whose name appears prominently in the history of the Crusades. His dynasty was, in turn, terminated when mercenary slave troops, brought in to serve as Egypt's defenders, took over and ruled Egypt until 1517. This period is called the Mamluk (which means "owned" or "enslaved") period because these rulers required that a person have the status of a slave in order to serve in the highest offices of the land. At times the Mamluk rulers, motivated in part by an effort to legitimize their rule in Muslim eyes, displayed a fanatical zeal for Islam. This effort caused suffering for Christians and, on occasion, even for Muslims. One such ruler even sought the approval of the Muslim leaders for expelling Christians from Egypt. He did not receive this approval because there was no Islamic basis for such an action.

Conditions did not change much under the Ottoman Turks, who conquered Egypt and ruled until 1798, when Napoleon Bonaparte invaded Egypt. Britain forced Napoleon out in 1801 and permitted the Ottoman sultan, after some struggles between the Mamluk and Ottoman officers, to designate Muhammad Ali as viceroy over Egypt. This began a dynasty that lasted until 1952.

Under the rule of Muhammad Ali, Christians fared well. He permitted them to attain high positions in the land and suppressed outbreaks of fanaticism. During his rule, Western missionaries began to arrive. His successor, Sa'id, abrogated the *dhimmi* status of non-Muslims, thus granting them equal citizenship. Isma'il continued these same policies.

Thus, the early nineteenth century marked a turn for the

better for Christians. They were increasingly sought out as artisans, physicians, engineers, accountants, and financiers. Muslims dominated politics and government, but Christians handled money and acquired land and education. Though they were despised at times, their fellow citizens generally acknowledged them as trustworthy. By any measure, until the mid-1950s, the number of Christians among the educated and cultured, the skilled and the wealthy in Egypt, was far out of proportion to their total number.

During the period of French control, division between the Muslim and Christian communities grew. Because Christians were forced to work for the French, they became identified with the infidel occupier. This led to the killing of some Christians by Muslims, followed by some Christian retaliation.

The most radical changes in the relationships between Christians and Muslims in Egypt occurred during the period of British occupation. In 1882, Britain established political hegemony over Egypt in order to force that country to repay the debts incurred while building the Suez Canal. The British remained in control of the canal until 1956, when Nasser forced them out of the canal area and full independence was gained.

The British hegemony over the affairs of Egypt enhanced the role of American and English missionaries. As did the French, the British used the skills of the Christians in the administration of the government. This fact, together with the presence of foreign missionaries, gave the Muslim observer the impression that Christians were colluding with and approving of the colonialists. In general, however, Christians were and are loyal to an Egyptian identity and nationalism. They participated with Muslims in political parties and in events that led to the revolt of 1919 and the subsequent establishment of a government independent, with some exceptions, of British control.

The constitution that was adopted in 1923 established a modern democratic government. It contained, however, two crucial provisions, one which provided that only a Muslim could be heir to the Egyptian throne and one which made Islam the state religion. These provisions were viewed by Muslims as not being substantively different from those in the English system of government, where the monarch must be an Anglican and the Anglican church is the state church.

During this period of relative independence owing to the vacuum created by the expulsion of the caliph by the Turks, many disputes arose relating to the king's ambition to become the caliph of Islam. His manipulations led to conflicts regarding the government's responsibility for the teaching of religion and for parochial school education. His ambition also contributed to the growing discrimination against Christians in the affairs of state and to internal conflicts within both the Muslim and the Christian communities. The continuing presence of foreign missionaries and British interference served also to increase misunderstanding and distrust between Egyptian Christians and Muslims.

It was during this same period, in the late 1920s, that Hasan al-Banna founded in Egypt the Muslim Brotherhood, an Islamic reform movement that focused upon moral and social purification, stimulated by a revitalization of Islam. The Muslim Brotherhood saw the impact of Western ways as an intrusion into the Islamic world and called for the establishment of an Islamic state under the rule of the Shari'ah law. For them, Christianity and Christians were a part of Western force. This movement has had a significant influence upon the whole Muslim world.

The Contemporary Scene

The revolution of 1952 that brought Gamal Abdel Nasser into power led to the establishment of a socialist republic and secured complete independence from the British. With this, the Christian community became increasingly marginal. The major disputes in Egypt occurred between Muslims on a wide variety of religious, social, and economic issues. At the heart of the religious questions was the role of Islam in the development of a modern nation. Though Nasser came into power with the support of the Muslim Brotherhood, he later was forced to outlaw the Brotherhood because of differences in understanding with respect to the role of Islam in the organization of the socialist state and the management of its resources, the meaning of Arab nationalism, and other matters.

During the Nasser regime, Christians found themselves separated from the positions of responsibility and authority within the government that they had enjoyed under the older party system. Some Muslim leaders and organizations also experienced this same separation. To make matters worse, various acts of violence were perpetrated upon the Christian community by some segments of the Muslim population, the reasons for which were not always clear but which have been understood by Christians as deliberately provocative and prejudicial to the welfare and interests of the Christian community. The complaints of the patriarch to the government evoked only a minimal response.

Two other issues confronting the Nasser government led to a strain in the relations between the two communities. The first of these was the continuing economic crisis, which thwarted constructive effort and gave rise to extreme political solutions. Within the context of those extreme solutions Christians often came under fire. Second, the Palestinian–Israeli war created major problems not only for the government (especially since Egypt was defeated in 1967) but also for the Christian community because, in spite of its protests to the contrary, it was viewed by some Muslim groups as part of a Judeo-Christian conspiracy against Islam.

This situation did not change much when Anwar Sadat came into power at the death of Nasser in 1970. Sadat began a cautious reform by allowing more freedom of speech and an "open door" policy with regard to investments. Once again the Muslim Brotherhood voiced its desire for an Islamic state and Islamic *da'wah*. The success of conservative forces in the Iranian revolution gave increased vitality to these concerns and efforts. This vitality created problems for both Sadat and the Christian community, and relations between them were occasionally problematic. Though he has since been freed, the internal exile of Coptic Orthodox Pope Shenouda III by Sadat was a low point for Christians.

The assassination of Sadat by Muslim extremists was a matter of deep concern for both Christians and Muslims. The present situation under Hosni Mubarak, in spite of many efforts, has not changed much, although Mubarak continues to be able to contain Muslim zealots. All this has important consequences for the Christian community, which is deeply concerned about its rights of full citizenship and future well-being.

Within the context of these events, the nature of the Christian community should also be kept in mind. The Christian community in Egypt today consists of the Coptic Orthodox Church, which is the oldest and largest community, the Roman Catholic Church, and the Protestant churches. The latter two communions are the results of the missionary enterprise of the Western church, and the great majority of their members have come out of the Coptic Orthodox Church. Within the Protestant community of some 245,000 people, the Synod of the Nile of the Evangelical Church of Egypt is the largest body, with a communicant membership of around 80,000, worshiping in some 270 congregations and 50 evangelistic centers. This Protestant community serves the larger society through social service programs and numerous educational and medical institutions. It has been among the pioneers in education for women, care of the aged, and schooling for the mentally retarded. Relationships between the Protestant community and the Coptic Orthodox Church are occasionally strained, and regular efforts are needed to reduce tensions.

Both the Coptic Orthodox Church and the Evangelical Church participate ecumenically in the worldwide church through the Middle East Council of Churches and the World Council of Churches. These ties have been used by some Muslims as evidence of the foreign character of the Christian community. To counteract this stigma, Orthodox and Protestant Christians have emphasized their national character and loyalties.

To summarize the state of relationships between Christians and Muslims in Egypt, several observations about the contemporary situation are useful. Relations between Christians and Muslims today are aggravated by a variety of factors: the severe economic problems of Egypt, the hurdles in the processes related to peace between Egypt and Israel and to the Palestinian–Israeli conflict, the increased vitality of movements for Islamic renewal and the rejection of Westernization, the struggles between Muslims over the nature of the state, internal struggles within the Christian community over that community's response to the current situation, and various forms of pressure from the outside that are exerted upon the Egyptian people and their institutions.

Though the broader relationships between Christians and Muslims are very precarious, there are some positive signs. In both communities there are many people of goodwill, some of whom have risked much for the sake of the other community. The government, aware of religious tensions and deepening fear, seeks to find adequate solutions. With this potential, there is hope for the effort to find those norms of justice and equality that are appropriate to Egypt's needs today.

THE UNITED STATES OF AMERICA

The growth of the Muslim community in the United States to over 3 million people is a significant aspect of American society today. Yet most Americans are not even aware of it. If they are aware, they know very little about it and interpret it mostly in terms of traditional Western stereotypes and prejudices, which are reinforced daily by much of the media, by some people in the U.S. government who are pursuing certain political objectives, and even by some missionaries and missionary agencies whose major concern is to make converts. In the United States this situation has led to the bombing of several Muslim mosques, the assassination of leaders who support Muslim or Arab causes, and numerous acts of discrimination and prejudice against Muslims and Muslim communities all over the United States. These attitudes and responses can be redeemed only by an attempt to understand something of the history of Islam in the United States and the character and

The full report upon which this condensation is based was prepared by William G. Gepford. His report included subreports prepared by C. Eric Lincoln, Yvonne Y. Haddad, J. Dudley Woodberry, and Otis Turner, all members of the Islamic Study Advisory Committee.

goals of the Muslim community as it endeavors to live in the pluralistic American society of today. This is an exciting opportunity because now, for the first time in American history, the American people are able to live and work with American Muslims directly, free from the biases of interpreters.

Islam Comes to the United States

Because of historical origins, the Muslim community in the United States may be divided, for analytical purposes only, into immigrants who arrived during the past eighty years and black Americans who came to Islam through the leadership of Elijah Muhammad and the "Nation of Islam."

Beginning in the late 1800s, immigration brought Muslims from Syria, Jordan, Lebanon, and Palestine into the Midwestern United States. Lacking proficiency in English, they became unskilled laborers in industrial centers or peddlers and merchants. Many expected to return to their native lands after they had earned their fortune. A great number stayed to become citizens. Those who did return encouraged other members of their families to emigrate. After World War II, immigrants reflecting the changing circumstances of the world, came from Palestine, Pakistan, and India. For the most part, they are professional people who have integrated well into the American professional scene and do not expect to return to their native country. A notable exception to this is that of the people of southern Lebanon who have immigrated, primarily to Dearborn, Michigan, as a result of the war in their area. Muslims of immigrant origins are now United States citizens, living everywhere in the country, with centers of population density in the major metropolitan areas. The earliest recorded group of immigrant Muslims who convened for prayer was in Ross, North Dakota, in 1900. The first building designated as a mosque was in Cedar Rapids, Iowa, in 1934. Since then about six hundred mosques or Islamic centers have been established, about two thirds of which belong to groups of immigrant Muslims. The Islamic centers in Washington, D.C.; Toledo, Ohio; and Quincy, Massachusetts, are notable examples.

That part of the Muslim community composed of black

Americans can trace its history back to the coming of Negro slaves to this country in the seventeenth century, as evidence points to the importation of thousands of African Muslims. None of the early Islamic traditions survived in any form except as a vague remnant memory within the black community. In the 1920s this memory emerged in the formation of a black organization called the Moorish Science Temple. The leader, Noble Drew Ali, sought by means of this movement to enrich black self-esteem by finding a black identity in the religion of Islam. By the 1930s the movement had lost its impetus. However, a few of the Moorish Science Temples remain today.

The concerns of that movement, including its orientation in Islam, were addressed by Wallace Fard, who initiated the group that grew in the 1930s into the Nation of Islam under the leadership of Fard's successor, Elijah D. Muhammad. This organization was successful in helping blacks deal with problems of racism and discrimination by means of an ideology that saw white society as Satanic and the Christian faith as Satan's religion and emphasized the need for blacks to find black solutions to the problems of unemployment and lack of educational opportunity, problems they saw as originating from the racist mentality of the white person. Islam provided only a kind of religious veneer for all of this, because the beliefs and practices of orthodox Islam remained unknown. Through Muhammad's efforts, however, Islam was brought to the consciousness of the American people.

In 1975, a major change occurred in the Nation of Islam when Elijah D. Muhammad's son and successor, Wallace D. Muhammad (now named Warith Deen Muhammad), introduced orthodox Islam into the life of that community. The black struggle for dignity and identity within white America is reflected in the subsequent changes in the name of the community, from the Nation of Islam, to the World Community of Islam in the West, and then to the American Muslim Mission. Finally the formal organization was disbanded in favor of finding an identity within the universal community of Islam. Imam W. Deen Muhammad remains as the unofficial leader of an informal association of some two hundred mosques, which were established by Elijah Muhammad in the Nation of Islam and which now have a membership of about 1.5 million people. Further, in keeping with Islamic teaching, the Christian faith and white people are no longer identified with Satan and white people are welcomed into the movement. A splinter group that challenges this change is led by Louis Farrakhan, Elijah Muhammad's former right-hand man, who wishes to remain faithful to the principles of black separation first enunciated by his leader. This group therefore claims to be the true successor of the Nation of Islam.

Muslim Organizations

The approximately six hundred mosques or Islamic centers located in almost every large city in the United States are the building stones of the community. Each has its own imam (the one who leads in prayers) and/or director, depending upon how the local community wishes to structure its community life In most of these centers Sunni and Shi'ah Muslims work together, though in some larger cities, such as Detroit, Michigan, where there is a significant Shi'ah Muslim population, there may be an Islamic center consisting wholly of Shi'ah. The division of mosques between the immigrant Muslims and the black American Muslims remains fairly distinct, but cooperation between them, including the integration of membership, is increasing.

As they assimilate into American society, the immigrant community has sought to address its needs through a variety of voluntary organizations. The Federation of Islamic Associations was established in 1952 to bring Muslims together from all over the United States at least once a year for education, reflection, and sociability. The Muslim World League, established by Saudi Arabia in 1962 as an international body for the promotion of the cause of Islam around the world, has a U.S. office in New York City.

Another very active organization, rooted in the immigrant community but gradually drawing black American Muslim centers into its membership, is the Islamic Society of North America (ISNA) with headquarters in Plainfield, Indiana. Founded in 1982, it has two foci: the Muslim community at large in the United States and the many Muslim students attending colleges and universities. With respect to this latter concern, ISNA is the successor to the Muslim Student Association and therefore seeks to address the needs of Muslim students.

There are several organizations that seek to bring together mosques and Islamic centers. The Council of Masajid, whose offices are located in the office of the Muslim World League, encourages cooperation among mosques in the United States and provides assistance in the construction, furnishing, and maintenance of mosques and center buildings. In the New England region an Islamic Council of New England has been established with offices at the Islamic Center in Quincy, Massachusetts. It is notable because the Islamic centers of both the immigrant and black American communities are united around the concern for the nurture of the community and the need for joint action with respect to the issues raised for them by the larger society.

Concerns of the Muslim Community in the United States

As it seeks to relate to American society, the Muslim community shapes its life so as to address several concerns. The major concern for all Muslims is to nurture the community in the belief and practice of Islam so that the community will retain its Islamic identity within American society and its members will hold fast to Islam. Christians who ponder their own identity in the secular society of the United States will understand the seriousness and complexity of this concern. Muslims attack this problem in slightly different ways. Though it is a generalization, one can say that immigrants are Muslims seeking to develop an American identity, whereas black Americans are Americans seeking to develop a Muslim identity. Ultimately both are working toward the same goal—an identity that is true to Islam and still appropriate to the cultural pluralism within which they live.

A second major concern for Muslims in the United States has to do with their experience of American racism and prejudice.

In general, the experience of the immigrant Muslim community has been that American pluralism and tolerance allow the community freedom to grow and propagate its faith. At the same time, the immigrant community experiences prejudice that is nourished by the stereotypes, the misrepresentations, that are directed toward Islam, Muslims, and Arabs. The prejudice is fueled by much of the verbiage of the media and of politicians as they interpret to the American public the complex issues relating to the Palestinian–Israeli conflict and to terrorism, and by Americans' fears of what has been represented to them as "Islamic fundamentalism." As a result, Muslim children have been harassed, mosques have been trashed or even bombed, and Muslim leaders have been assassinated. Ironically, it is this same American prejudice toward Islam which radicalizes many foreign Muslim students while they are in this country pursuing their studies. For the black American Muslim, this prejudice expresses itself in the racism that is a fact of life. It is expected that the more the American people retreat from a commitment to racial equality and justice in the United States, the greater will be the appeal of Islam to black Americans as they continue to look for alternatives that give meaning to life.

A third concern is related to the matter of nurture, but it also has other implications. This has to do with the rejection by Muslims of those aspects of the American secular life which they feel to be immoral and materialistic and which place an undue emphasis upon the welfare of the individual as opposed to that of the community. While appreciating the many freedoms enjoyed in the United States, they fear that the deterioration of religious values will lead to the destruction of a truly free society.

This leads to a fourth concern that is expressed by only a portion of the Muslim community who, in response to the American prejudice toward Islam, the social ills of this country, and the example of the conservative Christian missionary enterprises and because they are encouraged in their belief by the growth of a form of Islamic conservatism throughout the whole of the Muslim world, seek actively to convert Americans to Islam and in so doing to advocate the return of Islamic law.

The problems confronting America, they say, will be solved as Americans turn to Islam, because only in Islam are morality, social justice, equality among people, and a proper stewardship of the world's resources possible. Though reliable statistics are not available, evidence indicates that several thousand Americans every year convert to Islam. Most of these conversions do not appear to be the result of any focused "missionary" effort on the part of Muslims. A number of those Muslims who advocate "missionary" effort for conversions also call upon the community to refrain from association with the broader American society, except when work demands it, so that the community can retain its Islamic purity. The various ramifications of this concern are a subject of much debate among Muslims in this country.

Christian Organizations and Muslims in the United States

Within the context of the Christian missionary effort in traditional Muslim lands, American Christians have been associated with Muslims for over one hundred and fifty years. In this country, however, Christian awareness of a Muslim community in the United States is relatively recent, even though the study of Islam and the Muslim world has been in the curriculum of many colleges and universities since World War II. Hartford Seminary, building upon the work of its great Islamic scholar, Duncan Black Macdonald, established in 1975 the Duncan Black Macdonald Center for the Study of Islam and Christian–Muslim Relations. Assisted by the leadership of that center and of the World Council of Churches, the National Council of the Churches of Christ in the U.S.A. created its Office on Christian–Muslim Relations in 1977, with offices at Hartford Seminary. Both programs stand within the dialogue tradition of the World Council of Churches. This tradition affirms the Christian task of proclaiming the gospel but seeks to raise within the Christian church the question of how this mission should be conducted today. The specific focus of the Office on Christian–Muslim Relations is the relationship between Christians and Muslims in the United States, with its theological and practical implications. The office will assist any Christian, Christian church, or church agency to explore associations with Muslims in this country to learn about Islam and the Muslim world and their significance for the mission of the church. Further, it sponsors those cooperative activities that bring Christians and Muslims together in the pursuit of common objectives.

Christians have responded to the Muslim presence in the United States in other ways. In 1978, the Interfaith Conference of Metropolitan Washington (IFC) was established with membership from the Christian, Muslim, and Jewish communities. Centering its efforts on the social and economic conditions of the Washington, D.C., area, the IFC not only fosters religious tolerance but also brings the best insights of each tradition to bear on issues of social justice. In pursuing its concerns it is involved in a food bank program, a coalition for the homeless, medical services for the poor, a project on racism, and other efforts of a similar nature. Such interfaith work demonstrates that people of different religious backgrounds can live and work together when there is a spirit of trust, respect, and cooperation.

Another program through which Christians have sought to live and work in new ways with Muslims in a local situation is that which was established by the Presbytery of Detroit and the Littlefield Avenue Presbyterian Church of Dearborn, Michigan, in 1979. As a result of immigration patterns referred to previously, there are today over sixteen thousand Arabs resident in Dearborn, 90 percent of whom are Muslim. The Dearborn Arab community is a part of a much larger Metropolitan Detroit Middle East Community. In recent years this community has, as a consequence of the Palestinian–Israeli conflict, been greatly affected by an influx of Muslims from Lebanon. The Christian program seeks to assist the Arab community by providing various kinds of social services to the new immigrants, by developing those activities which will increase intercultural understanding between the older residents of Dearborn, both Arab and American, and the new immigrants, and by developing and/or participating in those interfaith structures that foster fellowship, cooperation, and dialogue.

Along with these programs, which have clear institutional identity, various church agencies are moving into the interfaith arena. In Wisconsin, the Ecumenical and Interfaith Commission of the Roman Catholic Archdiocese of Milwaukee has formed a Milwaukee Islamic–Christian Dialogue group. Similar efforts are being pursued by the Archdiocese of Los Angeles. Ecumenical councils in Buffalo, New York; Topeka, Kansas; Atlanta, Georgia; Los Angeles, California; and elsewhere are also at various stages in the process of incorporating Muslim participation in their life.

Reflecting other theological concerns, programs that emphasize the propagation of the faith beyond one's own boundaries have also been established. One such project that is supported by the Presbyterian Church is the International Neighbors project in Seattle. This project has focused primarily upon Muslim ethnic groups and seeks to provide opportunities to bring the two communities together and to offer learning about the Christian faith.

In a more focused concern, Christians of various church backgrounds, including some local Presbyterian churches, established in 1978 the Zwemer Institute of Islamic Studies in Pasadena. This center provides training in Muslim evangelism through a team approach, using the church-growth principles and strategies. It also is engaged in research on Muslim peoples all over at the world and, in conjunction with the Lausanne Committee for World Evangelization, organizes conferences and consultations on Muslim evangelization.

In addition to the various activities just described, many colleges, universities, and seminaries hold seminars, lectures, and panel discussions, with both Muslim and Christian participation, on subjects of mutual interest.

As contacts between the two communities grow, so also will the need for Christians to prepare themselves to deal with the issues that such contact will inevitably create. In the next chapter a number of these issues will be addressed in order to help Christians with this task. In addition to the foregoing observations, it is clear that the Muslim community in the United States will continue to grow and that Islam will continue to be an option for American people, especially if an erosion of values and ideals is associated with Christian failure. Finally, Christians and the church have a responsibility to be a voice of reason and a bearer of justice, reconciliation, salvation, and hope for all those who feel that they have been isolated, marginalized, or otherwise dehumanized as a result of their experience of American culture and American Christianity.

5

Issues of Theology and Practice

It is important to know which questions and issues are fundamental to mutual understanding and which are not. The preceding chapters have raised questions and identified issues; all are important, but some are more fundamental than others. This chapter will explore those questions of theology and practice which are crucial to an understanding of Islam, Muslim people, and Christian–Muslim relationships. No attempt will be made to provide a full or nuanced discussion of each question or to point out all the subquestions each issue spawns. The hope is that readers will discover and pursue these as they search for solutions to the fundamental problems.

In conducting this search Christians should be in constant and intimate conversation with Muslims. This conversation should be based upon a self-giving acceptance of the other person. It is a conversation carried on in humility and trust. From this kind of association, Christians will not only know more about Muslims and Islam, they will come to know some Muslims personally, as friends and fellow believers in God. Personal knowledge of people of another faith community, cooperative effort, trust, and respect will facilitate over the years ahead the discovery of answers to those problems that continue to disrupt efforts for peace and justice in the world. Such efforts also require constant return to the roots of one's own faith in an effort to discover on an even

---

This chapter was written by Byron L. Haines.

deeper level the meaning of Christian scripture and tradition.

Issues for Christian Theological Reflection

In the relations between Christian and Muslim, Christians must address several theological issues that have emerged as a result of continuing associations with Muslims over the centuries. These theological matters are complex and often emotional for Christians because they lie so close to the essentials of the Christian faith. In thinking about these questions, readers should also be aware that theological issues are never defended or discussed apart from the social, political, and economic convictions of each believer. Theology is not just a matter of scripture and creeds. Theological positions are also a response to the world, which makes them important. The world shapes the ways in which the Bible and the traditions of the church are interpreted. The implications of this awareness are very clear in the discussions of the theological issues and questions in Christian–Muslim relations.

The Question of Truth

As one studies differing religious beliefs, one learns that every religious tradition claims in various ways to be the only true religion. This gives rise to what scholars call "conflicting truth claims." Within the Christian tradition, this claim for truth is often justified in part by the biblical verse, "I am the way, and the truth, and the life; no one comes to the Father, but by me" (John 14:6). This verse lends itself to the attitude, "I have the truth. You don't. Therefore, you need what I have." When this attitude is embedded in a culture that considers itself superior to every other culture, the claim for truth becomes an exclusive claim. It produces attitudes of superiority and condescension toward those who are not so blessed. The question is whether this claim for truth in Christ is an exclusive claim. Does it mean that no other religion has truth about God? Are other religions able to witness to justice and righteousness?

The concern about truth can be put another way. Do Christians and Muslims worship the same God? The Islamic answer to this question is "Yes," because the Qur'an has revealed it to be so. The answer of the Christian church has been more ambiguous. The canon of the Bible was closed several hundred years before the Qur'an and does not mention Islam. The eighth-century church father John of Damascus said yes. Since medieval times, the greater portion of the church has said no. The fundamental issue can be put in this way: If people worship the same God, then are not both ultimately witnesses to the same source of truth? If such is the case, is the Christian claim that God is known only through Christ seriously challenged? In that challenge Christian feelings of superiority and exclusiveness are undercut. Any Christian interested in interfaith relations must accept this challenge and fashion a response.

The Question of Revelation

What people believe about God is directly related to what they understand to be revelation. In Christianity and Islam, God's self-revealing word is the form and substance of revelation. For Muslims, that word is the Qur'an; for Christians, Jesus Christ. Both, then, have by an act of faith committed themselves to particular understandings of revelation that differ from each other in both form and content. This difference is a fundamental issue in Christian–Muslim relations. The question about God is applicable to the two channels of revelation. Does the particularity of God's truth in one channel in itself rule out the possibility of God's truth being present in the other? For Muslims the answer, based specifically upon the Qur'an, is that the revelation given by God to Christians through Jesus (and by God to the Jews through Moses) is authentic, even though the record of such revelation has been distorted and corrupted by those to whom the revelation was entrusted. For Christians, the answer is more difficult. Jesus, who preceded the prophet Muhammad by some six hundred years, does not refer to Islam. For Christ, the authenticity of revelation was demonstrated in faithfulness to God's commands, not in abstract theological discussion. Where revelation encourages genuine faithfulness to God, its authenticity and truth must be acknowledged.

The commitment that Christians and Muslims each give to their own understanding of God's revelation is more than a question of truth or the validity of propositions. It is a question of obedience, loyalty, and faithfulness that give meaning and purpose to all of life. How one pursues issues of peace and justice (and many other matters) is directly related to one's understanding of what revelation requires. Take, for example, the matter of salvation. For Christians, salvation is the grace of God mediated through Jesus Christ. This salvation is what makes human life whole and complete. The Islamic concept of salvation stresses that the realization of a just and orderly communal and personal life is possible through obedience to the injunctions God has given in the Qur'an. In both cases, revelation is deeply involved with the way in which Christians and Muslims structure their societies. Does the existence of differing understandings of revelation mean that religious communities are forever alienated from one another? Is there within each understanding of revelation a similarity of truth sufficient to overcome alienation and to enable separate religious communities to make common cause in the pursuit of peace and justice and of faithfulness to God?

The Question of Mission

Theological discussion can become vexing because one question presupposes and leads to another. What Christians say about the revelation of God in Jesus has immediate implications for what is said about mission. Christians and Muslims both are obligated to witness to God's Lordship over the created world. This witness, if it is faithful to what God requires, invites others to walk in the same path. For Muslims, this witness is called *da'wah;* for Christians, the proclamation of the gospel or evangelism. Neither can avoid this witness and still be faithful. But if both revelations are from God, then is not the Christian imperative to witness to the salvation in Christ seriously diminished? What then becomes of mission? This is the theological aspect of the question of mission.

Another perspective is more practical but has theological implications. This side of the question requires sensitive listening to some complaints about the Christian missionary movement. As noted in chapter 4, a number of national Christian churches have objected to the proselytization of their members by Western missionaries, an activity facilitated by the economic resources available to the missionary but not to the traditional churches. The observations of Muslims move in other directions. They object to the disparaging and often untruthful way in which some missionaries have spoken about Islam and about Muslim people to weaken the faith of Muslims, making them more open to conversion. Some Muslims appreciate the educational and medical institutions operated by Western missionaries. They object, however, to the use of these institutions to attract Muslims into situations from which they cannot escape Christian preaching without losing the help they desperately need. Such proselytizing activity, they feel, is a form of compulsion. Finally, they see the presence of Western missionaries in their lands as a continuation of the colonial period, during which Muslims were ruled over and discriminated against by Western colonial powers. (Many Hindus and Buddhists would register the same objections.)

The person seeking understanding must investigate the ramifications of such criticisms. At stake is the meaning, motive, and conduct of mission. If the concern of Muslims to be faithful to God contains religious truth, then why do they need the Christian gospel? What are the motivations for mission? If the criticisms of the missionary movement are valid, does that mean that Christian mission should be terminated? Is there another way in which mission should be conducted? How is it possible to be faithful to Christ without falling into the arrogant superiority that has marred Christian–Muslim relations in the past? No solution will be reached easily.

The Question of Ecumenism

As interfaith contacts increase in the future, the meaning of ecumenism may also expand. In the past, to be ecumenical was to be concerned about the "unity of the church within the body of Christ." Today Jewish organizations and, in some few cases, Muslim organizations have been welcomed to full participation in local and regional ecumenical programs in the United States. Such associations suggest that Christians must consider the possibility that ecumenism should mean the "unity of humanity under God." If so, the practical significance of such a different theological understanding must be explored.

Issues for Christians and Muslims Together

The emphasis so far has been upon the questions and issues that Christians need to reflect upon with other Christians. There are many other concerns that Christians should discuss with Muslims. These concerns are common to both communities, although this commonality often goes unrecognized. Through such discussion Muslims and Christians will be less likely to assume that all of their problems are caused by the other. Christ's injunction to take the log out of one's own eye before trying to remove the sliver in the eye of another is much to the point here. What follows is an attempt to address the Christians' responsibility in the discussion.

The Question of Religious Identity

The first group of issues relates to the question of religious identity. Christians ask what it means to be a Christian in the world today and Muslims ask what it means to be a Muslim in the world today. The answer will inevitably be more than dogma. It will be shaped by ethnicity, national citizenship, culture, family roots, social mores, ethical standards, and economic status. The search for identity means for many Muslims the desire to have a national state in which the Shari'ah is normative. Adherence to this body of law, they believe, gives the community its identity as a Muslim community in contrast to the increasing Westernization that many Muslim countries are experiencing. Today many Muslims question the secularism and immorality of the West because they see these forces as threats to their identity.

Christians are, of course, raising the same kinds of questions from their own point of view.

The Question of Secular Ideologies and Mores

A second set of issues and questions focuses on the response of religious people to secular ideologies and mores as religious communities relate to the societies in which they live. Traditional societies feel the impact of Western culture and civilization upon the values they hold dear. Their appropriation of technology brings with it some aspects they perceive as threatening to their communal well-being and religious life. From the point of view of many Muslims and Christians in the Third World, the impact of Western technology and culture upon their societies has created many problems. For example, the introduction of modern medical practice has produced a population explosion in the Third World. As a result, Third World governments and communities are struggling to deal with the effect that increasing population has upon their economies, educational programs, political structures, and social values. Because Islam seeks to integrate all aspects of society, Muslim communities set many of these problems in a religious context.

Another example is the impact of secular scientific thought and technology upon traditional ways of understanding and interpreting life. In spite of the humanistic elements in modern thought and technology, it has often dehumanized people and values in the Third World. Technology makes people cogs in an industrial machine controlled by the technocrats of the West, along with their Third World counterparts. The Muslim response is often an attempt to prevent such dehumanization. Some in the West wrongly interpret this attempt as a rejection of advanced technology.

In the struggle to create modern societies, Muslims are not content to accept without criticism and alteration the Western ideologies of Marxist socialism or democratic capitalism. Rather, these ideologies are often viewed as extremes, with the Islamic alternative falling somewhere in the middle. The Islamic society addresses the same human needs and aspirations but seeks to avoid the oppressive excesses. In the totality of their lives, Muslims must first be faithful to God, because Islam is a total way of life. They believe that if this Islamic principle is upheld, they will be able to participate in the modern world in a way that incorporates the best of that world, rejects the worst, and is still genuinely Islamic. Such a vision helps Muslims to deal with social change within their own societies.

As these societies adapt to the Western world, the values advertised by television and movies, the widespread sale and use of pornographic literature, the extensive use of alcohol and drugs, and the tolerance of sexual license are seen by Muslims as threatening the social relationships and values that Islam enjoins. Muslims do not understand why these characteristics seem to have the tacit support of most Christians in the West. They also feel that Christian support of secular governments and the concept of separation of church and state contribute to the social ills manifest in Western society today.

The challenge of secularism is for Muslims more than a matter of social values and mores. It is a question of God's Lordship over the world. To the Muslim ear, Western ideologies seem to be saying that life can be lived without God. Science and technology can provide all that life requires. God is unnecessary because all human values and goals can be defined on the basis of individualistic hedonism. Social cohesion and cooperation can be achieved by an appeal to enlightened self-interest. As people for whom faithfulness to God is the central religious obligation, Muslims are understandably cautious about accepting such Western ideas.

Christians defend the secular character of the West as providing, in spite of its evils, freedom of opportunity and expression and freedom for life and faith not found elsewhere. Nevertheless they, like Muslims, are confronted also with the problems that secularism produces. The struggle with secularism is a common one. Christians and Muslims ought to be joined in working at it.

The Question of Social Justice and Human Rights

Many issues relating to social justice and human rights emerge from the long history of association between Christians and Muslims and from the events transpiring in the world today. Because the ethical positions taken by Islam and Christianity are, for the most part, similar, it was possible for representatives of both communities in 1948 to sign the United Nations' Declaration of Human Rights. Yet this document often stands in tension with what many believers feel that God commands them to do, especially when their lives are aggravated by violence, oppression, and violations of human rights inflicted by nations claiming to support the declaration. A major need is for Christians, Muslims, and Jews to determine a workable definition of human rights. As yet there is no process by which this understanding can be developed and implemented. Each religion offers a God-given set of social values and standards of conduct that claims the total obedience of its members. What happens, however, when the standards and values of one religion come in conflict with those of another? That is the subject of the following examples of situations involving differences in understanding of human rights. These examples demonstrate that in order to achieve peace and justice in a pluralistic society, there must be a process for dealing with differences.

Minority Rights

One specific issue is the concern for the rights and responsibilities of minority groups. Christians in the United States should be the first to admit that they have a poor record with respect to treatment of minority groups. The persistence of racism in the Christian church is evidence of this. In addition to racism, one must add the problems of anti-Arab, anti-Muslim, and anti-Islamic prejudices. These prejudices derive not only from the past history of Christian–Muslim relations but also from current slanted media presentations, the political rhetoric of national leaders, and the interpretations of Islam and the Muslim world found in many publications, including some Christian literature. Muslim citizens of the United States, while appreciating the freedom and opportunity afforded them, also ponder what their future might be in view of increasing prejudice and actions associated with it.

The other side of the coin is seen in the response of Christian churches in lands where Muslims call for the establishment of an Islamic state under the guidance of the Shari'ah. If Muslim governments implement this law, Christians fear they will be relegated to the status of *dhimmi*, or "protected people," the status provided by the Shari'ah for minority groups in a Muslim society. Even though under this provision the well-being of a Christian community would be guaranteed by the Muslim majority, Christian communities, as *dhimmi*, would not enjoy full citizenship as defined by United Nations standards. From both the Christian and Muslim perspectives, the rights of minorities is a crucial issue.

Freedom to Choose One's Religion

A second issue pertaining to human rights and social justice has to do with the right to choose one's religion. For Christians, the right to believe or not believe, as one chooses, without being compelled by any force or inducement (apart from the integrity of the religious message itself), is a basic human right. Islam maintains that in religion there can be no coercion (Surah 2:256). In practice, however, the right to choose has become confused and morally ambiguous. Both communities have at times sought to make converts by offering inducements, material as well as spiritual, and occasionally by force. Muslims claim that Christian missionaries use medical and educational institutions as inducements. These become a form of coercion because such offerings take advantage of the needs of people. Many Christians see the Islamic law against apostasy as a limitation upon the freedom of Muslims to choose their religion or to change it.*

The right to choose one's religious belief is, for both Christians and Muslims, closely associated with the obligation to witness to one's faith. Christians, therefore, engage in mission

---

*This law permits, after appropriate steps have been taken to give the apostate from Islam an opportunity to recant, the killing of the apostate. There is very little evidence that this law is normative throughout the whole Muslim world today. Rather, Muslims who convert to another religion are more likely to face social ostracism and be disinherited.

and Muslims in *da'wah*. Problems arise when religious communities fail to relate the obligation to witness to the right to choose. When this happens, one community may view as threatening the witness of another community within its midst. A majority community may deny the minority community full freedom to practice its religion. A community may seek in the name of God to restrict the freedom of its own members in such a way that their right to choose is denied. For these reasons and others, the right to choose one's religion, while affirmed in theory, still needs interpretation and discussion as far as religious practice is concerned.

The Rights of Women

The rights of women are an important concern with respect to social justice. Muslim and Christian women understand these rights differently. Today, many Muslim women feel that the status provided for them in Islam is superior to that enjoyed by women in the West. Conversely, many Western women feel that Muslim women are not granted their just due. In both communities, religious traditions, usually nurtured by men, have defined for women a role that is subservient to men. The pathways to liberation are therefore different for Christians and Muslims.

The rights of women are also associated with the role of the traditional family unit. Within Islam the extended family is viewed as the foundation of a healthy society. Muslim women see that as Western women gain more freedom to move beyond their traditional role, the family unit is weakened and the divorce rate increases. They are not sure that such changes would benefit their societies or increase their rights. Many Christians are concerned with the difficulties facing single-parent families that lack supporting communities. The breakdown of extended families has great significance for the future of congregations and communities as traditional structures disappear. Christians and Muslims, whether they like it or not, must address the rights of women as a matter of social justice.

Human Rights in the Middle East

To address issues related to social justice in a way that is meaningful to Muslims, Christians must at some point also discuss with Muslims the Middle East situation. Perhaps no one issue has done more harm to Muslim understanding and appreciation of the United States, no one issue has contributed more to the reaffirmation of Islamic identity, and no one issue affects Christian–Muslim relations more than the Palestinian–Israeli conflict. For Arab Muslims and Christians the displacement of the Palestinian people from their own land and the continuing violations of the human rights of the Palestinian people constitute an injustice that must be redressed. Arab Muslims and Christians believe that Christians in the United States are, through their government, giving support to unjust causes. They see this injustice emanating from Israel in partnership with the United States. The Israelis see their actions as sanctioned by their claim that God has given the land of Palestine to Jews and consequently by the right of Israel to exist as a Jewish homeland. Rather than becoming polarized around these issues, Christians in the United States need to understand both sides and work for justice with all parties in the Middle East.

In this discussion an attempt has been made to identify fundamental questions and issues. In addition, the place of religious teaching in public education; the rights of Muslims and Jews incarcerated in U.S. penal institutions; the American prejudice against Muslims, Arabs, and Jews; religious family law versus the secular family; and the need of Muslims and Arabs for protection against acts of violence should also be articulated. Many other concerns will surface as these basic problems are explored. The summary made in this chapter may help Christians to see that many of the issues confronting Muslims are not only religious but also human rights issues. Cooperative approaches and programs will provide the best answers and solutions. On the basis of this new understanding, there are specific directions that Christians can take which will invite constructive solutions. These directions will be outlined in the next chapter.

6

Directions for the Future

History and contemporary events, religious beliefs and obligations, feelings and emotions, political power and ambition, poverty and wealth, and many other factors are the warp and woof of the fabric of Christian–Muslim relations. Each factor in its own way both adds to and subtracts from the quality of the cloth, depending upon the care that is given to the weaving. With proper attention, the result becomes for Christians and Muslims the cloth of faithfulness to God, of reconciliation and peace. The weaving process that produces the cloth is a search in which all participants are engaged. It is a quest that suggests what the realistic expectations for the future might be. This search is a movement in three directions, each of which, though implicit and explicit in the preceding chapters, will be highlighted in what follows.

The Search for Understanding

Christians will not live well with their neighbors or with their responsibilities before God unless a measure of understanding prevails, an understanding that requires a knowledge of Islam, the Muslim world, and the relations of Christians with that world. This book has sought to provide that kind of knowledge. Real understanding, however, moves beyond data to personal association with Muslims. Understanding comes

This chapter was written by Byron L. Haines.

when we accept people as neighbors and not strangers. It means an involvement with Islam so profound that the Christian is able to appreciate and respect why some 900 million people choose to worship God in Islam.

Such understanding does not come easily. Old attitudes and patterns of activity are hard to shed, especially when the future seems so insecure. The reactionary movements present today in Islam and Christianity make this evident. As understanding grows, one sees that changes must take place, for the sake of the truth gained if for no other reason. With respect to Islam and the Muslim world, new understanding will produce in Christians a change in their attitude toward all people of other faiths. Such a change is needed if the stereotypes used to describe Americans, including American Christians, are to be overcome. The image of the "ugly American" extends to interfaith associations and must be dealt with. To change these stereotypes, Christians need a new attitude, an attitude that demonstrates in all aspects of life a genuine desire to love, respect, trust, and treat justly one's neighbor. They need an attitude of openness to and humility before another person, a willingness to hear and respect another point of view, and a desire to let other people be what they are, rather than attempting to make them like oneself as a precondition for friendship.

Such a change in attitude will greatly reduce the prejudice against Islam, Arabs, and Muslims that is manifested in the United States today by much of the media, by some of the statements of the nation's highest political leaders, and even by some Christian missionary organizations. This prejudice has worked its way into textbooks used in schools and even into some Christian education materials. Only by increasing understanding and changing attitudes can such prejudice be destroyed.

How similarities and differences between Christians and Muslims, between the Christian faith and Islam, are approached is also a part of this search for understanding. These similarities and differences are evidenced in theology and ethics, ideals and realities, history and contemporary events. They must be recognized and sorted out lest one or the other be distorted or unduly emphasized. Any discussion of similarities and differences between religious traditions should take into account four qualifications: (1) similarities do not necessarily lead to either syncretism or unity; (2) differences do not necessarily lead to either exclusivism or alienation; (3) depending upon the moment, the situation, and the person, any similarity or difference can be used as either a bond of unity or a wall of separation; and (4) unity of spirit and cooperation are more likely to emerge when points of agreement are stressed, whereas estrangement and rivalry tend to follow when points of disagreement are stressed.

These qualifications are given in order to make the reader aware of both the limitations and the possibilities that lie within any discussion of the similarities and differences of religious traditions. For example, Christians, Muslims, and Jews, each in their own way, identify Abraham as their "father." Because of this, some people today see this similarity as a common theological starting point for bringing the three religions together. The traditions within each religion that describe Abraham's significance are, however, different. At an earlier period in the history of interfaith activity, these differences were used by Christians as proof of Islam's heresy and need for correction. Does the similarity unite or does the difference divide? Which approach is the right one? What criteria have been used to make that decision? Such questions mean that the search for understanding should not be warped either by an unrealistic idealism or by pessimism. Interfaith concerns are not well served when similarities are stressed at the expense of differences, or vice versa.

The theological issues encountered in Christian–Muslim relations are of concern to Christians. No discussion of the search for understanding would be complete without some reference to them. Fundamental theological issues have been suggested in cnapter 5, but often Christians want more. Some want to point out the theological differences to show Christians why people should not believe in Islam. Some want to talk about theological bridges or similarities whose commonality may help bring Christians and Muslims together. There is extensive theological discussion of both kinds. Readers are encouraged to study these discussions because the results of such investigations do affect understanding. But where theological discussion leads will depend upon other assumptions that are derived from other sources, as well as upon the theological issues themselves.

Fortunately the search for understanding is much more than a discussion of similarities and differences or a challenge to rethink traditions and attitudes. It is a search to discover and know the inner nature of Islam and of the Muslim believer. For this reason, the best way to begin this search is to get acquainted with one's Muslim neighbors by including them within one's circle of friends. If such friendships are uncontrived, without ulterior motives, and based upon a willingness of both parties to accept each other as human beings, then there is hope for the kinds of living and working together that produce the deepest understandings and relationships. Since Christians and Muslims, in many places in the United States, do live next door to each other, Christians need to open their doors and invite their neighbors in.

The Search for Cooperation

Becoming a neighbor is essential to the search for understanding. Being a neighbor is the starting point in the search for cooperation. This book has to do with what it means for Christians to be neighbors to Muslims. The expectation is that in the act of being neighborly, there will develop between Christians and Muslims associations and activities that would not only benefit those involved but also be of some help to the larger community in which they both live. This is what the search for cooperation is all about.

Real cooperation begins with a recognition on the part of both Christians and Muslims that learning to live together is more important for faithfulness to God, for world peace and justice, than the perpetuation of alienation and enmity. If Christians take the position that the only way they can deal with people of other religious traditions and with the problems of the world is to make everyone a Christian, they will be disappointed. The history of Christendom contains much tragic evidence that Christians have acted inhumanely even against other Christians. The failure to live together as Christians is cause for humility, just as learning to live together with those of other faiths is cause for rejoicing. God's grace calls Christians to reconciliation that is the sign of faithful witness to Christ. Reconciliation, as the Presbyterian Confession of 1967 makes clear, is the basis of the peace and justice to which Christians are committed. For theological as well as pragmatic reasons, cooperation with people of other faiths is duty to which God calls the church.

For cooperation to grow, respect for the equality of all people before God and before each other must be present. To believe in the equality of all people before God implies, in human terms, that nations and societies should manifest, in all that they are and do, a belief in human equality, expressed by establishing the same social, political, and economic rights and privileges for all people. What belief in human equality means in theory and in practice is often quite different. Nowhere is the disparity between theory and practice more clearly visible than in the ethnocentrism and racism of the West. Many Christians recognize this problem and are trying to do something about it. Many other Christians do not. The disparity between the theory and practice of equality is seen in any society whose laws divide its citizens into different camps with disparate rights, privileges, and responsibilities. For this reason, Christians who live as minorities in predominantly Muslim nations are concerned about the enactment of any law that would take them out of the mainstream of the life of their nations or deprive them of any rights and privileges enjoyed by the majority. In either the majority or the minority situation, the absence of attitudes, laws, and customs based upon the principle of human equality make cooperation difficult except by the use of coercion. The search for cooperation between people of differing faiths becomes a search to implement in daily life the equality of all people under God.

This point is important for the kind of cooperative efforts that are slowly developing between Muslims and Christians within local communities all over the United States. People are not likely to enter into or support those activities if they are not full partners in every aspect of the effort. Activities that invite interfaith participation should provide for the equal involvement of all members in decision making and program planning. Compromise will be the order of the day. Agendas will include items that one member would prefer not to discuss. Items should be discussed even when supported by only a minority. The names of organizations that are involved in cooperative efforts will need to reflect fully the composition of their membership. Such changes are minor in view of the benefits of understanding and cooperation accruing to ecumenical and interfaith organizations that include people of other faith traditions as full partners.

What kinds of cooperative efforts can be undertaken? There are many, as indicated in the discussion of what is going on now in the United States. Certainly, any cooperative activity must be related to the concerns of those involved. The social and economic problems of the local community or region that have an impact upon both Christians and Muslims are important foci for cooperation. One major area of concern where cooperative action would be most beneficial at this time is the effort to eliminate the prejudice against and the stereotyping of Islam, Muslims, and Arabs. Such prejudice, when unopposed or unchallenged, breeds the violence and discrimination that has already occurred in the United States. If Christians are truly committed to the pursuit of justice, this cooperative effort is mandatory.

Other cooperative activities might be organizing study programs—for example, adult education events for churches and seminars or conferences for the community—involving both Christian and Muslim leadership and participation. The questions and issues in chapter 5 suggest topics for such study. Cooperative effort could also monitor community laws and procedures to be sure that they are nondiscriminatory and are applied equally to all religious groups. For example, in several cases zoning boards have ruled against an application to build a mosque in a particular location, whereas they have in prior actions approved building a church. Chaplaincy programs of federal, state, and local prisons could be monitored to be sure that the religious programs and dietary provisions are suitable to the religious practices of the prisoners. Developing community calendars that recognize officially the holidays appropriate to the religious traditions within the community could be pursued. Once attention is given to community problems, Christians and Muslims will discover other issues for common concern and action.

Though more activities could be suggested here, many such possibilities will be readily seen once the commitment to cooperation is pledged. Whatever is undertaken together, if it is appropriate, relevant, uncontrived, and without hidden motives, will enhance the search for cooperation. In such efforts all participants will grow in their understanding and appreciation of each other and their religious traditions.

The Search for Faithful Witness

In seeking understanding and cooperation, the question of motivation is central. This book has pointed to the existence in some Christians of an imperialistic attitude and behavior that Muslims have found offensive. Muslim objections arise not so much from what Christians preach about the Christian faith as from what Christians imply by their attitudes and behavior about Islam and Muslim people. A story is told about the stoning of a missionary preacher by his Muslim listeners in the bazaar of Peshawar, Pakistan, during the days of British rule. The records of the British police commissioner show that the Muslims said they stoned the missionary because he was not telling the truth about Islam. The missionary was not stoned because he was preaching the gospel. He was stoned because he was apparently demeaning Islam before Muslims. Despite the noble motivation of the missionary the outcome was not the sharing the love of Christ, no matter how strongly intended. Today, Muslims still suspect any Christian overtures toward them as being motivated by an imperialism that rides roughshod over their deepest convictions. In view of this sensitivity, it is imperative that Christians be very clear and completely open about their motivation. For Christians this concern for motivation leads to a search for a Christian witness that is faithful to God and as unfettered as possible by human constraints.

For both Christians and Muslims, the commitment to witness faithfully to the God whom they worship is inescapable. Any proposal for relationships which suggests that this obligation be abandoned is unrealistic. In light of this divine obligation to witness to God's Lordship over the world, the right of both communities to make this witness, freely and without restraint, must be upheld. Integral to the right to witness is the right to choose one's religion without being compelled to do so or being prohibited from changing if one so desires. If these rights are not upheld, then belief in religious freedom is called into question and religion is in danger of being used as a tool by totalitarian interests.

There is far more to the search for a faithful witness than stating religious rights. The questions of what witness is and what activity witness requires also need serious study. The inquiry about the meaning of witness is an important question for Christians. Christians associate witness with the purpose of mission and the proclamation of the gospel. For Christians, witness is the affirmation of the truth that God has revealed to them through Christ. It is a saving truth that, they believe, gives all of life meaning and purpose. Following a parallel line of reasoning, Muslims believe that the truth that God has revealed to them imparts meaning and purpose to their lives. To believe that something is true leads directly to witnessing to that truth. The witness will be either implicit or explicit, an unintended or intended part of the believer's life. For this reason religious people are always witnessing to that which they believe to be true.

The question Christians need to address is, What constitutes a faithful witness or a faithful proclamation? The emphasis is on the word "faithful." The term "faithful" has to do with the character of a believer's response to that which God requires. The degree of faithfulness to God's call in Christ determines the nature of the person's witness. The paragraphs that follow will suggest how faithful witness comes about.

In reading the following material, one should not conclude

that the mission of the church or the effort to be faithful requires little human effort and activity. To be faithful means that Christians make every effort to put into practice that which God requires. Program planning and implementation, including strategies and goals, are all a part of seeking to be God's faithful servants. This human effort is, however, of qualified value. Just because Christians plan for mission and witness doesn't mean that such planning or its results are what God intends, even when every care is taken to be as faithful as possible to that intention as it is found in the Bible. This qualification is in line with Reformed theology, which recognizes that all human effort is corrupted by human sin. In order for it to be that which God desires, it must be redeemed by God. In the following discussion, that Reformed principle will be applied in an attempt to free Christian understandings of witness and mission from the mistakes of the past in order to explore the challenges of the future.

First, since people are not completely faithful to God in all aspects of their life, no witness will be completely faithful. Every activity and belief is inevitably marred by faithlessness. Christians need to remember this when considering the kind of witness they are seeking to make. Faithful witness must take into account the human tendency to distort and pervert those very things to which they wish to testify. For this reason the prophetic call to repent is particularly pertinent to Christians. Only when Christians are able to live as forgiven sinners will their witness have the potential of being faithful.

Second, Christians proclaim Christ not because of any judgment they make about their neighbor's commitment to God, but rather because they are motivated by the joy which God's love for them in Christ has wrought in their lives. Faithful witness is a natural outpouring of the joy that is at work within believers and, as such, can lead them to an appreciation and respect for both the similarities and the differences encountered in the human religious experience without being judgmental about the faith of the other person or the religious state of those who adhere to that faith.

Third, everything Christians do and say—the cultural baggage they carry with them, the values their societies reflect, the attitudes they reveal in personal conduct—everything contributes to or detracts from the character of the witness. The gospel is proclaimed not just by preaching but by the total character of Christian life. No matter how much importance Christians attach to the preaching of the gospel, the outsider hears their preaching only within the context of the whole character of the preacher and the church. The biblical verse, "By their fruits you will know them," reflects the criterion others apply to Christians as they seek to understand what the Christian faith is all about. The search for understanding and cooperation with Muslims becomes, in the most inclusive sense, an essential part of faithful witness.

Fourth, many American Christians are eager to find clear and positive results from their witness to Christ. This passion for results can seriously compromise faithful witness. Faithful witness is never a result that can be achieved by setting goals, developing strategies, using statistical analyses, and planning programs. On the contrary, the more this witness focuses upon the measurable human achievement of strategic activities and goals, the less likely it is to be faithful, since human ways ultimately are not God's ways. Human activities, though a response to God's will, are always of transient value. They can and must be discarded or changed if the situation so advises. Patterns of mission that alienate, that exploit another's weakness, that treat other human beings as objects to be manipulated, or that ignore their own cultural baggage and impact must be discarded. They should be replaced by new patterns that seek to take into account the mistakes of the past, the needs of the present, and the realities envisioned for the future.

Fifth, whether or not a witness is faithful depends upon God's conversion of unfaithful human effort into that which is faithful. To the outsider this faithful witness is observed in the same way that one observes, when the conditions are right, the jet stream made by an airplane. It is God who made the conditions right for the jet stream. The pilot did not plan for the jet stream. Faithful witness is like the jet

stream. It emerges through the power of the Holy Spirit uncontrived, unplanned, unannounced, from the passing of
Christians who are going about their work in a way that is
faithful to God.

Finally, when witness is faithful, it invites reflection and
meditation on the power of God at work in this world. A life
that is faithful before God is invitational. It is an implicit invitation for the observer to turn to God. The life itself is only a
sign pointing to that which lies beyond or to the joy which is
at work in it. A faithful witness does not "make converts"; it
extends an invitation, not by a program designed to achieve
that end but as an unpremeditated offshoot of the obedient life.
The call to become a disciple of Jesus comes not from what
human beings are capable of doing but from what God is able
to do in and through human effort.

Within the context of the relationships between Christians
and Muslims, Christians and Muslims are both involved in
acts that make a witness. In view of the revelation that God
has given, such a witness cannot be avoided. It should be a
witness that is faithful to God. The search for a faithful witness entails at least the considerations that have been outlined
—and more. Christians, together with Muslim friends, are in-
vited to ponder what this "more" might be as they seek to be
obedient to God.

This chapter has pointed to new directions Christians might
take in their concern to live with Muslims as neighbors. These
directions have been described as searches for understanding,
cooperation, and faithful witness. By taking these directions,
Christians will discover new possibilities for the future of their
life together with Muslims. Perhaps, also, Muslims will be able
to understand not only why Christians do what they do or
intend to do in their relationships with Muslims but also why
they do it in their particular way. Throughout the book, very
little reference has been made to dialogue. That is because
everything said here is what dialogue is all about. The basic
motivation behind this endeavor is the desire to love God by
conforming to God's will by loving one's neighbor as one
loves oneself. Where this will lead and how it will bring Chris-

tians and Muslims together lies in the mercy and grace of God. Both Christians and Muslims live with the assurance of that mercy and grace. For this reason they both have hope that in the future their common life will manifest a faithful witness to God and provide for this world the peace and justice that faith nurtures and human beings so desperately need.

Glossary

dar al-harb   The house of war or conflict; the areas of the world not yet subdued by Islam

dar al-Islam   The house or abode of Islam; the true domain of Muslim faith and practice

da'wah   The call to faithful obedience to God; used by some to identify Muslim "missionary" activity

dhimmi   The protected status afforded to non-Muslim communities in an Islamic state, whereby such communities are guaranteed the right to complete religious, administrative and political freedom within the larger Muslim community, in return for their loyalty and the payment of a reasonable tax that will be utilized in the defense and administration of the state

hadith   The collected written reports of the non-Qur'anic traditions concerning Muhammad's sayings and deeds

Hajj   The pilgrimage to Mecca; the fifth pillar of Islam

Id al-Adha   The yearly feast of sacrifice which ends the ritual of the Hajj and which remembers Abraham's willingness to sacrifice his son, Ishmael, whom God replaced by a sacrificial animal; the most important of the two major Islamic festivals

Id al-Fitr   The yearly feast of fast-breaking, celebrating the end of the month of Ramadan; the second of the two major Islamic festivals

ijtihad	The exercise of independent judgment by legal experts whereby a consensus of the community is reached on a given legal matter
imam	The one who leads the community in prayer at the mosque
Islam	Submission and commitment to the will of God; the faith, obedience, and practice of Muslim people; the final, perfected, religion of God
jihad	Struggle or effort on behalf of God, mistakenly called holy war; the struggle against evil within the believer and the defense of the community against attacks from without
khalifah	The successor to the Prophet as ruler of the faithful; viceregent of God on earth (caliph)
Mecca	The holiest city of Islam, accessible only to Muslims; site of the Kaaba, the black stone
mosque	The place or house of prayer; the English translation of the Arabic word *masjid*
Muslim	One who practices or is a doer of Islam; one who submits to the will of God
Pancasila	The five pillars or principles which guide the policies of the Indonesian government
Qur'an	The holy book of Muslims, which was revealed to the Prophet Muhammad by God; the eternal word of God
Ramadan	The name of the month of fasting
salat	Worship in the form of prayer, five times daily; the second pillar of Islam
sawm	Fasting, abstaining from food, drink, sexual intercourse during daylight hours in the month of Ramadan; the fourth pillar of Islam
Shahadah	The bearing of witness to the unity of God and the prophethood of Muhammad; the first pillar of Islam
Shari'ah	The way or the divine path of true obedience to God; the large body of legal tradition which informs the community about the nature of the faithfulness that God requires of it
Shi'ah	Muslims who belong to that part of the total Mus-

	lim community whose traditions go back to Ali, the fourth caliph
Shi'ite	The anglicized singular form of Shi'ah
shirk	The act of association; any act of putting someone or something on a par with or ahead of God; idolatry
Sufi	An Islamic mystic
Sufism	Islamic mysticism
Sunnah	The path of the Prophet Muhammad; the Prophet's behavior, which is the standard of conduct for the community
Sunni	A Muslim who follows the Sunnah; a term which refers to the great majority of the Muslim community as distinct from the Shi'ah
Surah	A chapter in the Qur'an
tawhid	The assertion of the unity of God
ulama	The learned scholars of Islam; the custodians of Islamic teachings
ummah	The whole community of Islam; the community that God creates out of those who do Islam; in a general sense, the Muslim community in any locality
zakat	Almsgiving; the third pillar of Islam

Selected Bibliography

The purpose of this short bibliography is to suggest, in addition to those already indicated in the footnotes, other books on Islam, the Muslim world, and Christian–Muslim relations that are valuable for general reading.

Ariarajah, Wesley. *The Bible and People of Other Faiths.* Geneva: World Council of Churches, 1985.

Christians Meeting Muslims: WCC Papers on Ten Years of Christian–Muslim Dialogue. Geneva: World Council of Churches, 1977.

Cooley, Frank L. *The Growing Seed: The Christian Church in Indonesia.* New York: National Council of the Churches of Christ, 1982.

Cracknell, Kenneth. *Towards a New Relationship: Christians and People of Other Faith.* London: Epworth Press, 1986.

Cragg, Kenneth. *The Christian and Other Religion: The Measure of Christ.* London: Mowbray & Co., 1977.

Eaton, Charles Le Gai. *Islam and the Destiny of Man.* Albany, N.Y.: State University of New York Press, 1985.

Esposito, John L., ed. *Islam in Asia: Religion, Politics and Society.* New York: Oxford University Press, 1987.

Al-Faruqi, Isma'il R. *Islam.* Niles, Ill.: Argus Communications, 1979. Dr. Faruqi addresses this book to Western Christians.

Haddad, Yvonne Y., and Adair T. Lummis. *Islamic Values in the United States: A Comparative Study.* New York: Oxford University Press, 1987.

Haneef, Suzanne. *What Everyone Should Know About Islam and Muslims.* Chicago: Kazi Publications, 1979. A presentation of Islam by an American convert.

Irving, Thomas B. *The World of Islam.* Brattleboro, Vt.: Amana Books, 1984.

Murad, Khurram. *Way to the Qur'an.* Leicester, England: Islamic Foundation, 1985.

My Neighbor's Faith—And Mine: Theological Discoveries Through Interfaith Dialogue. Geneva: World Council of Churches, 1986.

Nasr, Seyyed Hossein. *Ideals and Realities of Islam.* Boston: Beacon Press, 1975.

———. *Science and Civilization in Islam.* New York: New American Library, 1968.

Nazir-Ali, Michael. *Islam: A Christian Perspective.* Philadelphia: Westminster Press, 1984. The perspective is that of a Pakistani Christian.

Newsletter of the Office on Christian–Muslim Relations. Hartford: Office on Christian–Muslim Relations—National Council of the Churches of Christ, 77 Sherman St., Hartford, Conn. 06105. An occasional publication available without cost to those who request it.

The Qur'an: The First American Version. Translation and Commentary by T. B. Irving. Brattleboro, Vt.: Amana Books, 1985. The first translation by an American convert to Islam.

Qur'an: The Glorious. Translation and Commentary by Muhammad M. Pickthall. New York: Mostazafan Foundation of New York, 1984. The standard English translation, also available in other editions.

Rahman, Fazlur, *Islam.* 2nd ed. Chicago: University of Chicago Press, 1979. The best single-volume presentation of Islam in English but written for advanced students.

Robinson, Francis. *Atlas of the Islamic World Since 1500.* New York: Facts on File, 1982.

Savory, R. M., ed. *Introduction to Islamic Civilization.* London: Cambridge University Press, 1980.

Speight, R. Marston. *Christian–Muslim Relations: An Introduction for Christians in the United States of America.* 3rd ed. Hartford: Office on Christian–Muslim Relations, 1986. (See address under *Newsletter.*)

Swidler, Leonard, ed. *Religious Liberty and Human Rights in Nations and in Religions.* Philadelphia: Ecumenical Press, 1986.